The Christian & Idolatry

A Study Consisting Of (1) A Tribute To The One True God, (2) An Examination Of The Psychological Nature Of Idolatry, And (3) A Critique Of Some Of The Idols We Moderns Have Constructed For Ourselves

Allan Turner

THE CHRISTIAN & IDOLATRY
© 2006 by Allan Turner

Published by Allanita Press

Cover design by Steve Sebree, Moonlight Graphics
Printed in the United States of America

ISBN 0-9777350-2-8

All rights reserved. No part of this publication may be reproduced, stored in a retrieval system, or transmitted, in any form or by any means, electronic, mechanical, photocopying, recording, or otherwise, without prior written permission.

For information:
Allanita Press
4324-A County Road 200
Corinth, MS 38834

Most Scripture quotations are from the Holy Bible: New King James Version, Thomas Nelson Publishers © 1964, 1965, 1966, 1971, 1975, 1983. Used by permission.

Dedication

To all those true New Testament Christians who are endeavoring to faithfully live in the difficult and complex *now* between the *then* of what they once were and the *not yet* of what they shall be in that magnificent glory of the new heavens and new earth.*

> *"Nevertheless we, according to His promise,
> look for new heavens and a new earth in
> which righteousness dwells."
> —*2 Peter 3:13*

The Cover Art And Its Meaning

The hands are from a fresco, The Creation of Adam, that was painted on the ceiling of the Sistine Chapel by Michelangelo *circa* 1511. The entire fresco is arguably one of the most famous images in the world. Michelangelo's depiction is intended to represent man's effort to illustrate the nature of man created in the image of God, in that God's right arm is outstretched to impart the spark of life from his own finger into that of Adam, whose left arm is extended in a pose mirroring God's. Famously, Adam's finger and God's finger are separated by only a slight distance. However, such anthropomorphism is viewed by many, especially non-Catholics, as the very essence of idolatry. At the same time, I cannot deny that the closeup of the fingers almost touching reminds me of the apostle Paul's statement in Acts 17:26-28, which says: *"And He has made from one blood every nation of men to dwell on all the face of the earth, and has determined their preappointed times and the boundaries of their habitations, so that they should seek the Lord in the hope that they might grope for Him and find Him, though He is not far from each one of us; for in Him we live and move and have our being, as also some of your own poets have said, 'For we are also His offspring.'"* But on the other hand, the very idea that something conceptualized by man can adequately depict the Almighty God clearly fits the definition of idolatry and has, no doubt, fueled the icon worship that is so prevalent in Catholicism. Thus, it is my belief that the art depicted on the cover of this book aptly serves to illustrate the sometimes complex and difficult to discern relationship that exists between the Christian and idolatry.

Table Of Contents

Preface 9

An Introduction: Ode To The Unknown God 11

God With A Capital "G" 17

Idolatry: A Category Of Unbelief 39

The Sham Gods Of "Orthotalksy" 55

The God Who Doesn't Do Anything 59

The God Who Doesn't Know The Future 75

The God Who Can Fail 93

The God Who Can Cease Being God 101

The God Who Must Be Either Here Or There 111

The State: A Mortal, But Very Supreme, God 127

Scientism: Modernity's Sacred Cow 149

Modern Churchanity, The God Of "Nice,"
And The "Age Of The Earth" Controversy 161

The "Only In And Through The Word" Bunch 179

Modern-Day Shibboleths 189

Our Theological Chickens Are Coming Home To Roost . 195

Index 201

Preface

From a very early age, I remember being interested in the nature and characteristics of God. I was especially interested in His omniscience, particularly His foreknowledge, and how it relates to man's free will.

Many think the foreknowledge of God and the free will of man are incompatible. Frankly, I never saw the problem that many see when thinking about these two things.

However, it was not until much later in life that I decided to do some in-depth study on the subject. As a result, it became even clearer to me that there was no conflict between God's foreknowledge and man's free will. But because this was not so evident to many of those around me, I wanted to know why.

While living and working in Kenya, East Africa in the early nineties, I decided to devote some time to thinking about the attributes and characteristics of God and how they relate to the subject of man's free will. It soon became apparent to me that far too many Christians were trying to relate to God as a man, albeit a man of larger proportions.

As I continued to think about the various ideas and concepts about God I had heard among my fellow Christians, I came to understand that many—and I do not exclude myself—frequently constructed and bowed down to a god (notice the use of the little "g" here) that was not the I AM THAT I AM revealed in Scripture.

I observed that this was being done by gospel preachers as well as, otherwise, knowledgeable Christians. These seemed to be unaware that they were regularly engaged in idolatry. It wasn't the pagan idolatry that one reads about in the Old and New Testaments, but it was idolatry nevertheless.

The book you now hold in your hand is a result of the study mentioned above. I, too, am only human and cannot point to any direct inspiration. Therefore, what I have written must be carefully viewed in light of the truths taught in God's word, the Bible. I ask only that you read what I've said with an open mind. If the ideas you find expressed here are unscriptural, illogical, or otherwise in error, just disregard them or take me to task. On the other hand, if you find truths here, then I implore you to make the adjustments in your own thinking that such truths require.

Finally, it is my prayer that this book might serve in some small way to bring the much deserved glory and honor that belong to Jehovah Elohim, the only true and living God.

Allan Turner
Corinth, Mississippi
July 2006

Chapter 1

An Introduction: Ode To The Unknown God

"You are My witnesses," says the LORD, "and My servant whom I have chosen, that you may know and believe Me, and understand that I am He. Before Me there was no God formed, nor shall there be after Me. I, even I, am the LORD, and besides Me there is no savior. I have declared and saved, I have proclaimed, and there was no foreign god among you; therefore you are My witnesses," says the LORD, "that I am God. Indeed before the day was, I am He; and there is no one who can deliver out of My hand; I work, and who will reverse it?" (Isaiah 43:10-13).

Some years ago I had a written discussion with a very capable brother on the subject of God's foreknowledge. It was during this discussion that I started to understand that, as incredible as it sounds, "THE UNKNOWN GOD" the apostle Paul spoke of to the Athenians in Acts 17 could be a God almost as unknown to Christians as He is to most pagans. If you think this a bit rash, I ask you to consider the following.

During the discussion, my esteemed brother used several human analogies in an effort to prove God could not know the future, contingent, free will choices of His creatures. These were the "master of chess" God and "God as novelist or playwright." In his master-of-chess analogy, his point was: "God does not need foreknowledge of the contingent free will choices and actions of men in order to bring His purpose to pass." He argued that "a master of chess would not need foreknowledge of a novice's moves in order to decisively defeat him." He then applied this analogy to God by arguing, "So it is with God and men." When using the God as novelist or playwright analogy, his point was that if God already knew the future, then it would have to be because He had already written it.

I pointed out to him that the problem with all such analogies is the inherent assumption, even when one is unconscious of it, that God is just a man of larger proportions—something the Bible categorically denies.[1] My objection to such reasoning was twofold: (1) the obvious effort to make God in the image of man, something Romans 1:23 clearly identifies as idolatry; and (2) God's foreknowledge cannot be legitimately compared with man's writing of a novel or play because God's foreknowledge, contrary to that of the novelist/playwright, need not be any more manipulative than omnipotence, an attribute my opponent readily admitted God could use to carry out His will without stomping all over the free moral agency of His creatures.

However, and this was a point that greatly offended my opponent, there is, in reality, little difference between the theologian's constructs (viz., God as a novelist or playwright analogies) and the pagan's idols—they are all substitutes of God. Further, when one insists on playing around on the slippery slopes of higher anthropomorphism he ought not to be so surprised when he falls victim of his own dubious assumptions. To this line of reasoning, my opponent said: "I am accused of an 'obvious effort to make God in the image of man,' and, therefore, of idolatry. This is a mighty serious charge to bring against a brother." I think I can understand how he must have felt, but I was obligated to show that ideas do, in fact,

---

[1] See Numbers 23:19 and Romans 11:33.

have consequences.[2] At issue was not whether I had made a serious charge against a brother, but whether the charge was true. Now, like then, I do not believe this brother knowingly involved himself in idolatry. However, he engaged in it when he superimposed man's imperfections and inabilities onto God. This, after all, is what idolatry is.

I refer to this incident not because I wish to embarrass or be unkind to my opponent in that debate, but because I think it serves to illustrate a weakness we Christians have when it comes to the subject of idolatry. It seems we have a tendency to think idolatry is something that only affects heathens. However, the tendency to idolatry is as prevalent today as it ever was. The Bible makes it clear that idols are not just concrete images found on pagan altars, but they can exist as false concepts in the hearts and minds of well-educated moderns, as well.

In the New Testament, the apostle John warned Christians to keep themselves from idols.[3] The apostle Paul wrote that Christians are to flee idolatry.[4] Are these warnings to all Christians throughout all time, or are they, as some claim, just warnings to Gentile Christians who were surrounded by pagan idolatry? Doesn't the Bible teach that all Christians are susceptible to covetousness? And doesn't this same Bible clearly teach that covetousness is, in fact, idolatry?[5] If so, then the Bible teaches that idolatry can affect modern "civilized" Christians, just as it did the ancients, and that we moderns must continue to be careful not to become entangled in its snare.

---

[2] See Proverbs 23:7.
[3] See 1 John 5:21.
[4] See 1 Corinthians 10:14.
[5] See Ephesians 5:5 and Colossians 3:5.

The Almighty Is A Jealous God

The true and living God, the One who has revealed Himself in the Scriptures, is a jealous God. As such, He demands that we have no other gods before Him.[6] Therefore, when we study Jehovah's revelation of Himself in the Bible, we must work very hard not to misunderstand what He says. If we do misunderstand—or worse yet, misrepresent—Him in any way, we could easily be entangled in idolatry. For example, I have heard people say, "The God I worship could never send anyone to Hell for an eternity." They go on to say that their God is a God of love, not wrath; mercy, not vengeance, *et cetera*. I believe most Christians will recognize the idolatrous nature of such thinking, for it is clear that people who talk like this have created a god (i.e., a theological construct or idol) who is much different from the God who has revealed Himself in the Bible. Consequently, all Christians, especially gospel preachers, must be very careful to understand correctly, and teach accurately, the magnificent attributes and characteristics of the Almighty God, Jehovah Elohim. When a preacher says that it is impossible for God to foreknow the future—unless He has acted to cause it to happen—simply because it hasn't happened yet, he is portraying, even though unintentionally, a god quite different from the One who has identified Himself in the Bible. And as I pointed out in the aforementioned debate, this is nothing less than idolatry.

The fact that the brother in that debate thought my mentioning of idolatry to be too harsh in a discussion between Christians is, I am convinced, indicative of a general misunderstanding of the far-reaching significance of idolatry. Idolatry is not just something

---

[6] See Exodus 20:1-2.

that pagans engage in; it is something Christians can, and do, participate in, as well. Therefore, an examination of idolatry—*what* it is and *how* it affects us—is a study that can be extremely helpful.

Our plan for doing so is as follows:

- *First*, we'll take a little closer look at the one true God who has revealed Himself in the Bible.

- *Then*, we'll examine idolatry itself, particularly its psychological nature.

- *Finally*, we'll consider some of the idols we moderns have constructed for ourselves.

The study will be challenging, maybe even taxing, but when we're through, I hope you will agree with me that it was worth the effort.

Chapter 2

God With A Capital "G"

You shall have no other gods before Me (Exodus 20:3).

God with a capital "G," the "I AM THAT I AM," is that one and only[1] state of being God, consisting of the Father, Son and Holy Spirit—a state that is like no other: self-existent, eternal, infinite, and immutable.

A proper understanding of this God is absolutely necessary. In fact, salvation and true worship are not possible without the proper knowledge of *who* and *what* God is.

I know this is true because when Jesus prayed for His disciples, He said, "And this is eternal life, that they may know You, the only true God, and Jesus Christ whom You have sent."[2] In other words, one's eternal destiny depends upon knowing God, the Father, and His Son, Jesus Christ. This means that the study of God and Christ cannot be ignored by those who want to go to heaven.

In addition, other passages inform us that the Holy Spirit is to be included in this intimate, knowledgeable relationship.[3] Consequently, it should not seem strange that upon a confession of one's faith in Christ Jesus, a penitent believer is baptized into a relationship with the entire Godhead, Father, Son and Holy Spirit.[4] All who enter into this relationship are said to "Know the

---

[1] See Deuteronomy 6:4.
[2] John 17:3.
[3] Acts 5:32, for example.
[4] See Matthew 28:19.

Lord,...from the least to the greatest."[5] And finally, "when the Lord Jesus is revealed from heaven with His mighty angels, in flaming fire," He will be "taking vengeance on those who do not know God."[6]

True worship, which is the only kind that is pleasing to God, must be in both spirit and in truth.[7] This means that true worship must not just be with the right attitude or spirit, but it must be intelligent and knowledgeable as well. For example, although there were many reasons why the Samaritan woman's worship was not acceptable to God, the primary reason was stated by Jesus, when He said, "You worship that which you do not know."[8] In the same manner, the Athenians vainly worshipped at the altar of "THE UNKNOWN GOD." The Bible makes it clear that this kind of worship is unacceptable because it is "worship without knowing."[9]

It is sad that modern society knows very little about the one true God. According to Langdon Gilkey, in his book, *Maker of Heaven and Earth*, the prevailing picture of God, among those in our culture who still believe in Him, is that of "a large, powerful, kindly elder statesman who treats us much as a doting grandfather might do, with occasional moods of needed judgment but with a balance of indulgence."[10] Add to this the fact that many Christians, reflecting the ignorance of God so prevalent in our day, are, like the ancient Athenians, attempting to worship an "UNKNOWN GOD," and you have the potential for a major apostasy brewing in our midst.

---

[5] Hebrews 8:11.
[6] 2 Thessalonians 1:7,8.
[7] See John 4:24.
[8] John 4:22.
[9] Acts 17:23b.
[10] Page 81.

If what I am reading in the religious papers can be trusted, and if preachers and elders I have spoken with have a sense of what is happening in their midst, then too few Christians today study their Bibles on a daily basis. It would be my guess that fewer still have ever engaged in a private study of the nature and person of God. If this is true, then many Christians know very little about God's attributes and characteristics. Such ignorance is, according to an inspired apostle, a "shame,"[11] and dare I say, "disgrace." Just as a lack of knowledge about God made the Corinthians susceptible to false teaching about the resurrection, many Christians today, knowing little about the nature of God, are vulnerable to vain philosophy and empty deceit.[12]

Having, therefore, placed this study in its proper perspective, it is now time to turn our attention to a study of God the Creator, Sustainer and Redeemer of the world.

God Is...

The Psalmist, in Psalm 19:1, said, "The heavens declare the glory of God; and the firmament shows His handiwork," and the apostle Paul, in Romans 1:20, said it this way, "For since the creation of the world His invisible attributes are clearly seen, being understood by the things that are made, even His eternal power and Godhead, so that they are without excuse."

With these scriptures in mind, it is interesting to note that, down through the ages, men who were not even associated with the Bible have looked at God's magnificent creation and have understood there must be a Creator. This realization is called "the teleological argument for God," and is the argument from design,

---
[11] 1 Corinthians 15:34.
[12] See Colossians 2:8.

inferring an intelligent designer of the universe, just like one infers that a product (viz., a watch) has a producer (viz., a watchmaker). For example, if someone were to show us a watch, telling us that no one made it, but that it was the result of an explosion that had taken place accidentally in a scrap metal factory, we would think that person was either "pulling our leg" or mighty foolish. Why, then, should it be any different when we think about the greatest product ever created? In fact, the Bible says, in Psalm 14:1, that "The fool has said in his heart, 'There is no God.'"

According to Plato, one of the things that makes one believe in the Creator is the argument "from the order of the motion of the stars, and of all things under the dominion of the mind that ordered the universe."[13]. According to him, there had to be a "maker and father of all." In addition, Aristotle, based upon his observation of the creation, concluded there had to be a First Unmoved Mover who is God, a living, intelligent, incorporeal, eternal, and most good being who is the source of the order in the universe.[14]

In making note of the observations of these two men, I wish to make it clear that I am not advocating their philosophies. Instead, I am simply pointing out that the greatest minds of antiquity understood the force of the teleological argument. As the Bible so plainly says, in Romans 1:20, man is "without excuse" for not knowing that God is.

...Self-Existent

The God who has revealed Himself in nature and gradually, verse by verse, step by step, makes Himself known in His special revelation, the Bible, is a necessary being who depends on nothing

---

[13] Plato, *Laws*.
[14] Aristotle, *Metaphysica* and *On Philosophy*.

else or anyone else for His existence. In fact, everything else depends on Him. This means that God, ontologically speaking,[15] is self-existent. This is the meaning of the name "I AM THAT I AM" recorded in Exodus 3:14. It derives from the Hebrew verb "to be" and means "He who is." It is this self-existence that is the primary point of difference between God and His creation. Therefore, in calling Himself "I AM," God is arguing, ontologically, that His being is *uncaused*. He is saying that He *is*; *always has been*; and *always will be*. In other words, God's being is not derived from anything, and is not dependent upon anything; He just exists.

There are three New Testament passages that convey this same idea. In Romans 1:23, God is identified as being "incorruptible." In 1 Timothy 6:16, it is said that God "alone possesses immortality." And in John 5:26, it is taught that only God "has life in Himself." When God's self-existent nature begins to be comprehended by finite creatures, they feel the need to humble themselves before the totally independent and incorruptible I AM.

...Eternal

If God is self-existent, and this is clearly what the Bible says, then He must also be eternal. In fact, belief in the Eternal is an essential part of the Christian's faith.[16] And although it is true that the creature will one day put on immortality and live forever, according to 1 Corinthians 15:53,54, this is not the immortality that God possesses. God, contrary to His creation, is immortal by nature. In other words, only God *has always* existed and *will always* exist. How can this be? How can a being have no beginning and no end? How can it be that a being always was and always will be?

---

[15] Having to do with the *being* of God.
[16] See Hebrews 11:6.

Because, as we have already pointed out, God *alone* is self-existent, and a logical consequence of this self-existence is eternalness.

For the creature, immortality is a gift. But for God, immortality is the very essence of His nature. As finite creatures, our minds are controlled and limited by time. Consequently, it is impossible for us to fully understand the eternalness of God's nature. So, as we stand before Him in awe, we reverently say, along with the apostle Paul: "Oh, the depth of the riches both of the wisdom and knowledge of God! How unsearchable are His judgments and His ways past finding out!"[17] And surely we join with Moses in saying that the "eternal God" is our refuge, "and underneath are the everlasting arms."[18]

God, then, has a unique existence. In addition to being self-existent and eternal, He is not limited by anything outside of Himself.

...Infinite

This kind of existence is referred to as being infinite, which means *subject to no limitation or external determination* (i.e., unbounded). But one needs to be careful with this word. As Jack Cottrell points out in his book, *God The Creator*, when referring to God as infinite, this term is not to be understood in its physical or mathematical sense, as if God were infinitely large, or as if He extended infinitely into space.[19] To say that God is infinite, is to say that He is not subject to the built-in limitations of a created being.

---

[17] Romans 11:33.
[18] Deuteronomy 33:27.
[19] Page 241.

...Omnipresent

God's infinitude is to be defined by His self-existence, eternalness and omni-characteristics, which are omnipresence, omniscience, and omnipotence. The God who is eternal, and therefore not limited by time, is omnipresent and not limited by space.[20] He is universally present to all of space at all times. Even so, this does not mean that He is dispersed throughout the infinite reaches of space, so that every part of space has at least a little part of God. God is not present *in* all space; He is, instead, present *to* all of space. This means that the unlimited God in His whole being is present at every point of our space. But perhaps a better way to express this is to say that all space is immediately present before God.

With this in mind, it must be understood that God's omnipresence does not prevent Him from manifesting Himself in a localized place. In fact, although His ontological being is present to all of space equally, He has, at various times, entered space at specific points and become present in it for a specific purpose. These "theophanies," as they are called, most often involved redemption. For example, the pillar of cloud bearing the glory of God that appeared before the Israelites is but one example of such a case.[21] Of course, the most dramatic incident of God entering time and space was the incarnation itself.[22] Consequently, Jesus was called Immanuel, or "God with us" in Matthew 1:23. But, in entering time and space, God, in His self-existent, eternal and infinite Being, did not cease to be omnipresent. He was, in fact, still present to every point of space, holding everything together by the "word of His power."[23]

---

[20] See Psalm 139:7-10; Proverbs 15:3; Jeremiah 23:23,24.
[21] See Exodus 33:9; 40:34; 1 Kings 8:10ff.
[22] See John 1:14; 1 Timothy 3:16.
[23] Hebrews 1:3; cf. Colossians 1:17.

In fact, it is evident that the omnipresence of "God with us" is the subject of John 3:13, which says, "No one has ascended to heaven but He who came down from heaven, that is, the Son of God who is in heaven." If omnipresence is not under discussion in this passage, then pray tell me what is? Remember, these words were being spoken by God Himself while enfleshed here on this earth. Another example of God interjecting Himself into time and space would be the coming of the Holy Spirit on Pentecost,[24] as well as His indwelling of the body of every Christian.[25] "Mind-boggling," you say. Yes, but such is the magnificent nature of the great I AM.

...Omniscient

When one considers passages like Isaiah 46:9-10, Psalm 147:5, Romans 11:33, and 1 John 3:20, one comes to appreciate the fact that there never was a time when the self-existent, eternal and infinite God of all creation knew less or more than He does right now. God, because of who He is, never learns and never forgets. This characteristic is called omniscience. Omniscience is not anything like the knowledge man possesses. Man, by his very nature, cannot know some things. God, on the other hand, knows all things,[26] and does so because He is "He who is."[27]

Nevertheless, some are willing to argue that there are things that even an all-knowing God cannot know. These argue that the future free will acts of men and women cannot be known by God because they have not yet happened. God, according to this position, cannot know what cannot be known, and the future,

---

[24] See Acts 2:1-4.
[25] See 1 Corinthians 6:19.
[26] Consider 1 John 3:20.
[27] Exodus 3:14.

contingent, free will choices of men and women cannot be known. But can this be true? What is it that the self-existent, eternal, and infinite God cannot know? There is, of course, absolutely nothing that such a Being could not know, for He transcends the flow of time and sees the past, present and future in a kind of eternal now. Only a being with the infinite characteristics and attributes of God could be all-knowing. Consequently, it is omniscience that the capital "G" God uses to challenge those who claim to be gods (all the little "g" gods), but who are, in fact, no God.[28] Surely, praise, honor and eternal glory belong to the one and only true God who said, in Isaiah 46:9 and 10, "I am God, and there is none like Me, declaring the end from the beginning, and from ancient times things that are not yet done."

...Omnipotent

Since God is self-existent, eternal, omnipresent and omniscient, it comes as no surprise to us that He is also omnipotent or all-powerful. In fact, if God is infinite in His relationship to time, space and knowledge, it only follows that He is omnipotent as well. In the New Testament, this truth is taught in Matthew 19:26 and Revelation 19:6. In Genesis 17:1, when God appeared to Abraham, He said, "I am God Almighty." In Jeremiah 32:27, He says: "Behold, I am the Lord, the God of all flesh. Is there anything too hard for Me?" For God, of course, "nothing [consistent with His nature] is impossible."[29] Finally, God's omnipotence, according to Jeremiah 32:17, is grounded in the fact of creation: "Ah, Lord God! Behold, You have made the heavens and the earth by Your great power and outstretched arm. There is nothing too hard for You."

---

[28] See Isaiah 42:8,9; 43:3-7; 44:7,8; 45:20,21; 48:3-7.
[29] Luke 1:37.

...Immutable

Given the nature of God, there is no chance that He can ever be anything other than what He is. This can be inferred from His self-existent, eternal, and infinite nature. His nature or essence cannot change, but is eternally the same, incorruptible[30] and immortal.[31] In other words, He is unchangeable or immutable.[32] What does this mean? It means that the Self-Existent One cannot be *not* self-existent; it means that the Eternal One cannot be *not* eternal; it means that the Infinite One cannot be *not* infinite; *et cetera, et cetera, et cetera*. God, ontologically speaking (again, by the nature of His being), cannot be anything else other than *who* and *what* He is—if He were, He would not be God.

Included in God's unchangeable or immutable nature are His moral attributes, for His moral character is no less a part of His essence than are His power and wisdom. What this means is that God has always been, and always will be, the holy, righteous and gracious God that He is at this moment. His goodness has not been developed and will never be altered. From everlasting to everlasting, He is the same in character, infallible and immutable.[33]

Of course, it must be kept in mind that the immutability of God's nature does not mean that He cannot interact with His creation. In fact, the Bible teaches that the Almighty has agreed to, and does, interact with His creation within the bounds of time. Such interaction is genuine and not pretended. God has agreed to be influenced by His creation. Whether or not I can explain this in view of God's immutable nature is not the point. I cannot even

---

[30] See Romans 1:23.
[31] See 1 Timothy 6:16.
[32] See Psalm 102:25-27; Malachi 3:6; James 1:17.
[33] See Numbers 23:19.

understand it; how, then, can I explain it? In truth, it is not my responsibility to explain it; it is, instead, my responsibility to believe, teach, and defend it. If I had to be able to understand and explain everything about God, especially those things He has not chosen to reveal to me, before I could believe in Him, I and every other finite creature could have no choice but to remain in unbelief. The Aristotelian, or classical, view of God as "the Unmoved Mover," who is, in turn, unrelated to the world, impassive and unconcerned, is, in my opinion, as ridiculous as it is un-Biblical. As such, it reflects idolatry, pure and simple.

As I've said, it is not possible that the essence of God could be anything other than what it *has been*, *is* and *always will be*. If this essence were to change, then God would no longer be God. As a matter of fact, it is impossible to make distinctions between God, His essence, and His attributes. "I AM THAT I AM" or "He who is,"[34] exists as a *self-existent*,[35] *eternal*,[36] *infinite*,[37] *immutable*[38] *Spirit*.[39]

If God ceased to be any of these, He could not be the capital "G" God. In other words, God's essence (i.e., that which makes Him what He is) could not be anything other than what it is; and that which makes God what He is, of course, is His attributes. Therefore, it is never correct to think of God apart from His essence or attributes. Namely, God does not have an essence; He *is* His essence, and He does not have attributes; He *is* His attributes. For example, the Bible tells us, in 1 John 4: 8 and 16, that God is love. It

---

[34] Exodus 3:14.
[35] See Romans 1:23; 1 Timothy 6:16; John 5:26.
[36] See Deuteronomy 33:27.
[37] See Psalm 139:7-10; Isaiah 46:9,10; Jeremiah 32:27.
[38] See Psalm 102:25-27; Malachi 3:6.
[39] See John 4:24.

further informs us that God's love is *great*,[40] *eternal*,[41] *infinite*,[42] and *dependable*.[43]

If the theme of the Bible is man's redemption, and it is, then the central word of the Bible is love. In fact, the Bible tells us that the motivation for the scheme of redemption is God's love for His creation. How much did God love His creation? He loved it so much that He was willing to give His only begotten Son so that it could be redeemed.[44]

But, what kind of love would do such a thing? To understand this, we must realize that God's love for mankind is a distinctive kind of love called *agape* (pronounced *ah-gah-pay*). And what is *agape*? Primarily, it is good will toward others. It is deep, tender, and warm concern for the happiness and well-being of another; it is charity toward those in need.

Therefore, when the Bible says, "God loves us," it means He really cares about us and always does what is best for us. God's love is different from other kinds of love in that it seeks to give and not to get; it seeks to satisfy not some need of the lover, but rather the need of the one who is loved. This is what God is, i.e., this is His nature. Strip from Him His love and we no longer have the God who has revealed Himself to His creatures. Strip from Him His love and what remains is something similar to the little "g" gods of the pagans, which are nothing but "idols for their own destruction."[45]

However, what the Bible does not say about the essence or nature of God is just as important as what it does say. For instance,

---

[40] See Ephesians 2:4.
[41] See Jeremiah 31:3; Ephesians 1:4,5.
[42] See Ephesians 3:18,19.
[43] See Ephesians 3:18,19.
[44] See John 3:16; 1 John 4:9.
[45] Hosea 8:4.

although the Bible teaches that God is His attributes and characteristics, it does not teach that any particular attribute of God is God; i.e., the Bible is not saying, and has never said, that "Love is God." On the contrary, what the Bible teaches is that "God is love."[46] Clearly, then, the Bible instructs us that God is His attributes and characteristics, and anyone who believes the Bible believes this. Consequently, God *is*, *has been*, and *always will be* who and what He is at this exact moment.

...Triune

In the one state of being God,[47] there are three distinctly different personalities: the Father, the Son (or Word) and the Holy Spirit. Each one of these personalities shares fully the one essence, nature, or state of being God. Everything involved in being Deity is possessed by each of these personalities. In other words, the Bible teaches there is one, and only one, God; but it just as plainly teaches that the Father is God,[48] the Son is God,[49] and the Holy Spirit is God.[50] Even so, it must be understood that although the Bible says that God is three persons in one essence,[51] it does not teach "Tritheism" (i.e., three Gods). As Roy Lanier, Sr. wrote on page 46 of his book, *The Timeless Trinity*:

> *We do not affirm that one God is three Gods; we affirm that there is but one infinite Spirit Being, but within that one Spirit essence there are three personal distinctions, each of which may*

---

[46] 1 John 4:8,16.
[47] See Deuteronomy 6:4; Romans 3:30; 1 Corinthians 8:4.
[48] See John 6:27; Galatians 1:1; Philippians 2:11.
[49] See John 10:30; 20:28.
[50] See Acts 5:3,4.
[51] See Matthew 28:19; 2 Corinthians 13:14.

be, and is, called God; each capable of loving and being loved by the others; each having a distinct, but not separate, part to play in the creation and salvation of man.

We Must Be Very Careful With Our Human Analogies

I think it wise to caution that, when thinking of God, it is possible to use "person" or "personality" in a wrong sense. If we are not precise in our thinking, we might conclude that the three persons or personalities that are God are just like human persons or personalities, except more complex. This would be a common, but serious, mistake. Human personalities are totally different from each other, and their relationships are often inharmonious and completely external (i.e., they do not partake of the same essence). On the other hand, the three personalities that are God partake of one essence and are always harmonious. In other words, we must not try to think of divine personality within the limits of human personality, as if God were but a more complex image of the human person. To do so would be idolatry, pure and simple.[52] Consequently, one must not press too far the concept of personhood when applied to God. What, then, are we saying when we speak of God in three persons?

As has already been pointed out, divine personality is the archetype of human personality; it is not the other way around. If this is true, then there must be some similarities between divine personality and human personality and, in fact, there are. As Paul taught the Athenians, "Therefore, since we are the offspring of God, we ought not to think that the Divine Nature is like gold or silver or stone, something shaped by art and man's devising."[53] In other

---

[52] See Romans 1:23.
[53] Acts 17:29.

words, we are not lifeless, impersonal matter, and neither is God. The Bible teaches that God is Spirit, and therefore we who are His offspring have a spiritual nature. The Bible teaches that God is personal, and we who are His offspring partake of personhood. In his excellent book, *What The Bible Says About God The Creator*, Jack Cottrell, on page 237, points out four elements that are characteristic of personhood:

- rational consciousness,

- self-consciousness,

- self-determination, and

- the capacity to have relationships with other persons.

These characteristics are, in fact, a very intricate part of the portrait God paints of Himself in the Bible, from beginning to end. Based on Scripture *alone*, no one would ever doubt God's personhood.

If, then, the self-existent, eternal, infinite, and immutable Spirit has three personalities, and this is what the Bible teaches, then the Father, Son and Holy Spirit partake of personhood. As such, each enjoys rational consciousness, self-consciousness, self-determination, and relationships with other persons. This means that the Father is conscious of Himself as an individual person apart from the Son and the Holy Spirit and *vice versa*. It means that the Father, of His own free will, decided to send His Son into this world for the redemption of mankind. It means that the Son, of His own free will, responded positively to His Father's decision when He came to this earth and experienced death for fallen humanity. Finally, it means that the Holy Spirit, of His own volition, came to this earth to do the bidding of both the Father and the Son. And although it must be understood that the Father, Son, and Holy Spirit were, and are, all involved in man's redemption, nevertheless, each person in the Godhead had work to do that was unique only to Him.[54] When one reads the Bible, these truths are clear. By clear, I do not mean that I think it is easy for finite creatures to understand how this *threeness* is rooted in the divine essence. On the contrary, by clear, I simply mean that the doctrine of the triune nature of God is explicitly taught in the Bible.

The Economic And Ontological "Trinities"

Theologians speak of the "economic Trinity" and the "ontological Trinity." These are constructs that attempt to define God. The so-called economic Trinity refers to the "division of labor" that exists between the Father, Son and Holy Spirit, and concerns itself principally with the different works done by the three persons of the Godhead in relation to the scheme of redemption. For example, the Bible depicts God the Father as foreknowing and choosing the plan whereby man could be redeemed.[55] In His role (or work), the Father is never portrayed as being the One sent. On the contrary, the Father sends the Son and the Spirit.[56] In turn, the Holy Spirit is involved in the work of sanctification,[57] and He is also the agent of inspiration.[58] In this connection, it is interesting to note that it is *only* blasphemy against the Holy Spirit, and not against the Father or Son, that is unforgivable.[59] From this, one can clearly see that the three persons of the Godhead are truly distinct. It is, of course, the works of Jesus, the Son of God, which receive most of

---

[54] See 1 Peter 1:1,2.
[55] See Romans 8:29.
[56] See John 5:37; 14:26; 20:21.
[57] See 1 Peter 1:1,2.
[58] See John 16:13; 2 Peter 1:21.
[59] See Matthew 12:31,32.

the attention in the New Testament. This is because it is He who "became flesh, and dwelt among us."[60] It was only the Son who experienced death for us. It was only the Son who was resurrected from the dead, taken bodily into heaven, and seated at the Father's right hand. It is only the Son who is the High Priest and Mediator between God and man.[61]

Therefore, the Bible teaches that, when it comes to the scheme of redemption, there are works done by the Father that are not done by the Son or the Spirit; there are works done by the Son that are not done by the Father or the Spirit; and there are works done by the Spirit that are not done by the Father or the Son. It is this Bible-based division of labor or economic Trinity that sheds some light on the so-called ontological Trinity.[62] Discerning a threeness in the external manifestations and works of God is not too taxing, but when one turns his attention to the ontological Trinity, things begin to get a lot harder. For instance, are the appellations of Father, Son and Holy Spirit eternal distinctions within the Trinity, or are they derived from the various works of God in the scheme of redemption? Particularly, from the standpoint of the Scriptures, is the doctrine of the eternal Sonship of Christ authentic? For example, Alexander Campbell taught that Jesus Christ, according to John 1:1, pre-existed as the Divine *Logos* or Word of God, but that His Sonship began with the incarnation. According to Campbell, the entire "relation of Father, Son and Holy Spirit began to be" during the days of Augustus Caesar.[63] Personally, I am not certain that the eternal Sonship of Christ is Biblical and, furthermore, I do

---

[60] John 1:14.

[61] See 1 Timothy 2:5; Hebrews 4:14.

[62] Namely, how the three persons of the Godhead are related within their own being, totally apart from any manifestations or works directed outside themselves.

[63] *The Christian System*, pp. 9-10.

not really see what difference it makes. There are several explicit references to the Deity of Christ in the Bible; consequently, His Deity (or equality with God) does not depend on an eternal Sonship relation.

But how, then, do we explain the ontological Trinity? Personally, I do not think we can with any large degree of specificity. When we do try, we seem to fail, and fail miserably. Furthermore, many attempts to explain or depict the ontological Trinity (i.e., three in One) actually incline toward idolatry,[64] which is something we should be seeking to avoid with a passion. We must always remember that God is not a man; therefore, He cannot ultimately be explained or understood by trying to compare Him with finite creatures. And although it is absolutely impossible for three finite creatures to consist of the same essence, nevertheless, God, who is three Divine persons, and Who is identified in the economy of redemption as the Father, Son and Holy Spirit, is also, and at the same time, one self-existent, eternal, infinite, immutable Spirit Being.

There can be no doubt that the Biblical doctrine of the Trinity transcends the limits of our finite knowledge. By reason *alone*, and by this I mean reason unaided by divine revelation, we cannot figure out the ontological Trinity. But by concentrating on the economic Trinity revealed to us in the Bible, we can know what the Triune God wants us to know about Himself. Consequently, I agree with professor B.B. Warfield, who concluded, "When we have said these three things, then—that there is but one God, that the Father and the Son and the Spirit is each God, that the Father

---

[64] See Romans 1:22,23.

and the Son and the Spirit is each a distinct person—we have enunciated the doctrine of the Trinity in its completeness."[65]

Mythology is filled with numerous triads, but there is only one Triune God. And if it had not been for the scheme of redemption, we would know very little of His *threeness*. In fact, although there are allusions in the Old Testament that the Godhead consists of more than one person, if Scripture had not depicted Jesus of Nazareth as God incarnate, and the Holy Spirit as Deity, the question of the Trinity would have never arisen. This means that Jesus Christ and the Holy Spirit are the fundamental proof of the doctrine of the Trinity. This means that if the pre-existent Jesus (i.e., the Word or Divine *Logos* of John 1:1) actually divested Himself of His Godhood and Divinity, so that the "fullness of the Godhead" did not dwell in His earthly body,[66] as some are currently teaching, then the Triune God, who has identified Himself as a self-existent, eternal, infinite, immutable Spirit, ceased to exist as He had existed, at least for a period of time. Therefore, one can readily see that the current controversy over the Deity of Christ being manifested in churches of Christ is not a "tempest in a teapot" issue; but is, instead, an issue that strikes at the very core of the gospel. With this in mind, it is now time to turn our attention to the Biblical truth that there never was a time when the Divine *Logos* was not God with a capital "G."

Jesus Is God

This is the basic meaning of the incarnation. In John 1:1, the Holy Spirit teaches that not only was the Word (i.e., the *Logos*) in

---

[65] "The Biblical Doctrine Of The Trinity," in B.B. Warfield, ed., *Biblical And Theological Studies*, pp. 22-59.
[66] See Colossians 2:9.

the beginning *with* God, but the Word *was* God. In verses 14-34 of the same book, we learn that the *Logos* became flesh in the person of Jesus of Nazareth. And in this book that was written so that men would believe that Jesus is the Christ, the Son of God, and believing might have life in His name, Thomas, speaking of Jesus, exclaims after seeing Him in His resurrected body, "My Lord and my God."[67] There are, of course, other passages that directly speak of Jesus as God, but since they are all disputed by some, I have chosen not to mention them here. Nevertheless, the passages cited serve to demonstrate, to those who are willing to believe the Bible, that Jesus is, in fact, God.

Furthermore, the writer of Hebrews, telling us what God had prophesied about Jesus, writes, "But to the Son He says: 'Your throne, O God, is forever and ever.'"[68] Also, he clearly identifies Jesus as the Jehovah and Elohim of Psalm 102:25-27, who eternally existed before He created the heavens and earth,[69] and who remains eternally the same,[70] and who is, in the person of Jesus Christ, "the same yesterday, today, and forever."[71] To see in Hebrews 13:8, as some do, only a reference to the faithfulness of Jesus, and not a reference to His immutability, is a serious mistake. In fact, Jesus Christ's faithfulness is grounded in His changelessness. In other words, because He does not change ontologically (i.e., because He has always been the fullness of God that He is at this very moment), He has been, is, and always will be, completely and totally reliable. It is only in this sense that Jesus could identify Himself as the "I AM THAT I AM" or "He who is" of Exodus 3:14.[72]

---

[67] John 20:28.
[68] Hebrews 1:8.
[69] See Hebrews 1:10.
[70] See Hebrews 1:11,12.
[71] Hebrews 13:8.
[72] See also John 8:58.

When Jesus said, "Most assuredly, I say to you, before Abraham was, I AM," He used the *aorist tense* to describe Abraham's existence, but the timeless *present tense* to describe His own existence, and thereby identified Himself as the self-existent, eternal, infinite, immutable God with a capital "G." Well has it been said:

"Lord, You have been our dwelling place in all generations. Before the mountains were brought forth, or ever You had formed the earth and the world, even from everlasting to everlasting, You are God."[73]

As difficult as it may be for finite creatures to even begin to comprehend, when the Divine *Logos*, or Son of God, became flesh[74] or, as the Bible says elsewhere, came in the likeness of man,[75] or was manifested in the flesh,[76] He did not divest, give up, or have stripped from Him, His Deity. Within the man Jesus of Nazareth dwelt, and continues to dwell (for such is the meaning of the present tense), all the fullness of the Godhead bodily, as Colossians 2:9 so clearly points out. In fact, from a Biblical standpoint, the historical Jesus is never understood apart from His embodiment as the self-existent, eternal, infinite, immutable God in time and space. And although it is true that a God divested of His Deity would still continue to exist, in truth, He would no longer be what He had been and, therefore, could not call Himself "I AM THAT I AM."

Now, with a concept of the true God firmly imprinted in our minds, it is time to turn our attention to the various substitutes for God (viz., idols) that men invent.

---

[73] Psalm 90:1,2.
[74] See John 1:14.
[75] See Philippians 2:8.
[76] See 1 Timothy 3:16.

Chapter 3

Idolatry: A Category Of Unbelief

Beware, brethren, lest there be in any of you an evil heart of unbelief in departing from the living God (Hebrews 3:12).

An idol is a substitute for God. It is the exchanging of the truth of God for a lie.[1] All idols belong either to *nature* or *history*. There are no other areas to which man can turn in order to find a substitute god, for all creation ultimately falls into these two groupings. Consequently, idols that are not artifacts of the natural world are constructs of the social world (or history). As such, they serve no other purpose than to facilitate the worshipping and serving of the creature rather than the Creator.[2]

Furthermore, idolatry may be seen as a category depicting unbelief that is highly sophisticated, drawing together the complexities of motivation found in psychology, sociology and demonology. Of these, demonology is the most familiar, and most obvious. As this aspect of idolatry has been given extensive treatment over the years, I will not spend time with it here. Suffice it to say that the Bible teaches there is an unseen spiritual dynamic at work behind idolatry,[3] and although this is an important theme in the Bible, it is often neglected and misunderstood by many

---

[1] See Romans 1:25a.
[2] See Romans 1:25b.
[3] See 1 Corinthians 10:19-22.

Christians.[4] In this study, however, I want to concentrate especially on the psychological and sociological aspects of idolatry.

In Genesis 1:27-28, the Bible says God created man in His own image.[5] By virtue of his creation in the image of God, man lives out his life in two directions: (1) upward toward God, as he trusts Him as his Sustainer and Creator, and (2) downward in dominion over the rest of creation. Trusting in God, man is to subdue and exercise dominion over the earth and its creatures. This is the way God made us, and deep down inside us all, this is the way we are. In other words, these upward and downward directions of our lives are part of our psychological nature. When we understand this truth, we will be in a much better position to recognize idolatry in all its various manifestations. But before we can proceed any further, it must be made clear that something happened that sorely affected man's psychological nature.

Genesis, chapter 3, records the rebellion of Adam and Eve, along with the awful consequences of that rebellion. As a result, the world is no longer a safe place to live. Our plans to cash in on the good life are constantly being frustrated by disease, accident, theft, bankruptcy, rust, decay and, finally, death. Every graveyard stands as proof that instead of us subduing the earth, the earth now subdues us. The trust we place in this world is regularly betrayed as we pursue our illusions with extravagant expectations that are seldom, if ever, fulfilled. Finally, forced to live in an environment marred by sin, we are no longer strangers to anxiety and disappointment.

---

[4] See Ephesians 6:10-18
[5] This, incidentally, is why every attempt to make God in man's image is idolatry.

Sin did not eliminate the built-in psychological drive to worship God and exercise dominion over the rest of creation. It did, however, pervert it. Satan's seduction of Eve, and subsequently Adam, was through the "lust of the flesh, lust of the eyes," and "the pride of life."[6] Thinking "the tree was good for food, that it was pleasant to the eyes, and a tree desirable to make one wise,"[7] Mother Eve believed the Tempter's lie which said she could successfully be her own God, deciding good and evil.[8] As a result, she erected in her own heart an idol to SELF. Adam, on the other hand, was not deceived. Instead, he chose to follow his wife's lead,[9] erecting in his heart an idol of his WIFE. In the fall of these two people who were the prototype of the entire human race, the centrality of God was replaced with egocentricity. In short, the world no longer began and ended with God; instead, it ended with themselves.

As we think about the nature of Eve's rebellion, it helps us in our study of this subject. Her rebellion happened, at least in part, below the level of her own perception, in that she was, as the Bible says, "deceived."[10] This demonstrates that idolatry is not always as overt as some seem to think. It also alerts us to the deadly danger of self-deception that lurks in all forms of idolatry.

Because of his psychological nature, man is going to worship something, even if it is himself, as he tries to subdue or exercise control over creation. Therefore, when he engages in God-avoidance, rebelling against the Lord's moral precepts, the Bible makes it clear that he will inevitably turn to idols.[11] He will not just

---

[6] 1 John 2:16.
[7] Genesis 3:6.
[8] See Genesis 3:5.
[9] See Genesis 3:6a, 17.
[10] 1 Timothy 2:14 and 2 Corinthians 11:3.
[11] See Romans 1:18-32.

eliminate knowledge of the true God from his thinking, he erects substitute gods in His place. The Bible calls these substitutes "idols." Noting this, G. K. Chesterton observed that when we "cease to worship God, we do not worship nothing, we worship anything." In other words, when we refuse to worship the true God, we are busy building the shrines and temples of the substitute gods.

Although the Christian rightly rejects the Calvinistic doctrine of inherited depravity, he must nevertheless recognize that our acquired, sin-sick natures predispose us to act independently from God (i.e., to be laws unto ourselves). Exercising our own autonomy, we do exactly what we want to do without considering His Word. And, if we had not been originally created to be in a personal relationship with God, we could have dismissed once and for all the whole religious dimension of life and lived happily ever after, eating, drinking and being merry.[12] But made, as we are, in the image of God, and having an innate psychological need to worship and exercise faith in Him, we, when we manage to pervert ourselves with sin, try to deny our guilt feelings by eliminating in our minds the true concept of God, which in turn creates a vacuum in our hearts.

We then try to fill this vacuum with idols. As I've already mentioned, we do this by inflating things in nature and history to religious proportions. Therefore, an idol can be a physical object, a property, a person, an activity, a role, an institution, a hope, an image, an idea, a pleasure, a hero—anything that can substitute for God. It can be riches, pleasure, fame, power, et cetera. An idol can be things that, in and of themselves, are good, like work, recreation, family, et cetera, but when used incorrectly, causes us to

---

[12] See Luke 12:19; 1 Corinthians 15:32a.

disobey God out of our loyalty to them. An idol can be something as seemingly harmless as wanting to be well-liked, a perfectly legitimate and natural desire, if wanting to be liked means we never risk disapproval or criticism. Even something as good as foreign evangelism can be an idol, if the one engaged in it is willing to circumvent Bible authority to get the job done, or if he should be so presumptuous as to make his work the litmus test for foreign evangelism.

Idolatry always involves one in self-centeredness, self-inflation and self-deception. It starts with the counterfeiting of God, for it is only with a counterfeit god that one can remain the center of his life and the autonomous architect of his own future. Then, when such rebellion is complete, some thing or person is idolatrously inflated to fill the God-shaped vacuum left in the heart. Of course, the idol, whatever it may be, is not the real thing. It is only a counterfeit—a lie that promises the blessings of the so-called "good life;" but in the end, produces a debased and reprobate mind that spawns even more sin and degradation.[13]

In his fallen and sin-sick condition, man no longer trusts God; but as Chesterton pointed out, this does not mean he no longer trusts in anything. In order to authenticate his life and feel secure about himself, fallen man still feels the need to trust in something, whether it be a thing, idea, institution, or another person. This trust, divorced as it is from a proper faith in God Almighty, is perverted into overdependence on a thing, an idea, an institution, or another person, even when these things continually betray his trust. Nevertheless, out of his desperate need for authentication and safety, he desperately clings to his idols. In conjunction with this, the God-given, and therefore legitimate, need to subdue and

---

[13] See Romans 1:24ff.

exercise dominion over the creation is perverted by fallen man into domination, something quite different from what God originally intended. To enjoy the "good-life," sin-sick man thinks he must manipulate and dominate those around about him. This inevitably involves the controlling of certain key variables (often people) in his life and surroundings. All this (both overdependence and domination) is engaged in to assuage the anxiety created by fallen man's perverted psychological needs—needs that are, in turn, derived from the God-given needs to trust in God and exercise dominion over the rest of creation.

Idols Always Come In Pairs

Because this duality (viz., to trust in God and subdue creation) is so deeply imprinted in the human psyche, idols seem to always come in pairs. An idol, remember, is a counterfeit of the true God. It does not just substitute God's existence, but it can also exist as a counterfeiting of His attributes and characteristics. With this understood, it should be realized that God's transcendence can be made into one idol and His immanence into another. In the informative book, *No God But God*, edited by Os Guinness and John Seel, Richard Keyes wrote an excellent chapter entitled "The Idol Factory," in which he calls these two counterfeits "the faraway idol" and "the nearby idol."[14] These designations are not so much spatial as they are psychological. The far-away idol, who is intangible and therefore always inaccessible, serves as an overarching idea that gives meaning to all of life. On the other hand, the nearby idol, who is much more accessible and tangible, allows the idolater to manipulate his world so he can get what he wants. This

---

[14] 1992, pages 29-48.

construct is classic to idolatry, and is not just the key to understanding idolatry, but is essential to understanding the occult, as well. We'll explore this nearby idol first.

The Nearby Idol

When one has alienated himself from God, the nearby idol is a substitute for God's immanence. Because he is no longer dependent upon the blessings of his Creator to help him exercise stewardship over his environment, the idolater seeks a sense of well-being through control. The nearby idol, whatever the idolater conceives it to be, permits him to exercise this control. It is, of course, a delusion.

This is illustrated in the rebellion of the Jews who fled into Egypt contrary to the Lord's command.[15] It had been their custom, even when they were back in Judah,[16] "to burn incense to the queen of heaven and pour out drink offerings to her."[17] Of course, they were not doing this for nothing. In fact, they were deluded into thinking they were being blessed by their manipulation, through their sacrifices, of this counterfeit god.[18] They were wrong, of course. It was actually God who had been blessing them due to His longsufferingness. Finally, though, they started to experience God's punishment for their idolatry. However, it just so happened that this punishment coincided with the Jews ceasing to sacrifice to their false god. In turn, they mistakenly came to think they were no longer enjoying blessings because they had quit

---

[15] See Jeremiah 44:1-30.
[16] See Jeremiah 7:18.
[17] Jeremiah 44:17.
[18] See Jeremiah 44:18.

offering cakes to their idol, the queen of heaven. Grossly deluded, they believed their nearby idol allowed them to experience a certain leverage over the important forces that control life. Consequently, they were convinced that their fertility goddess was able to give them good crops, more livestock, and more male children. This nearby idol was all they needed to enjoy the good life, they mistakenly thought, but their devotion to this counterfeit god ultimately caused them to be consumed by the famine and sword of God's wrath.[19]

Although idolatry can't really deliver, polytheists/occultists believe that their rituals and sacrifices permit them to tap into, or connect with, invisible powers that will allow them to exercise control over the visible (or natural) world in which they live. To these devotees, the nearby idol, whatever it might be, is a means to some desired end, and to accomplish this end they are willing to genuflect to their substitutes gods and goddesses.

America's Carpet God

The nearby idol for many Americans is Carpet. "And what," you might ask, "is Carpet?" Carpet represents the comfortable home with its decorations, color combinations, furniture, appliances, and video/audio systems. Carpet is the "nice home" so many Americans think is essential if one is to experience the "good life." A multitude of Americans have bowed to Carpet. In doing so, they have demonstrated that they will sacrifice anything they have for the comfort Carpet promises. For example, think of the millions of "latchkey" children who come home to empty houses every school day who must fend for themselves because mommy

---

[19] See Jeremiah 44:27.

and daddy are too busy sacrificing to Carpet. These children are, in reality, a blessing from the true God who has, in turn, obligated the parents with certain responsibilities. Consumed with Carpet, multitudes of American parents ignore their God-given obligations to their children, but who cares? Unfortunately, not even some who call themselves Christians. Yes, they shudder at the thought of ancient Israelites sacrificing their children to Molech,[20] but then they turn right around and leave their children in the hands of perfect strangers or, worse yet, they cause them to fend for themselves while they both go off to work so they can obediently worship at Carpet's totem. It is most unfortunate that while the divinely ordained family structure is being offered up on Carpet's altar, many Christians just don't seem to care. Worse yet, some Christians are themselves worshipping in the shrine of this cruel and ogreish god. Like all idols, Carpet promises much, but is unable to deliver on anything of real value. The messages of the idols are all lies, and Carpet's message is no different. It promises safety and comfort from the troubles of life, but when trials and tribulations finally come, and they will, the Carpet god is completely powerless. Carpet cannot comfort us when we lose a loved one; it cannot be our friend when we are alone; it cannot help us when we are dying. Nevertheless, many believe Carpet's lies and, in turn, sacrifice everything, even their children, to worship at its altar. The Bible, which pulls no punches, says that covetousness, which is personified in Carpet, is idolatry.[21]

When we consider the nearby idols to which men bow, it is not hard to see the devastating effect they are having on our society. However, it is now time to turn our attention to the faraway idol.

---

[20] See Jeremiah 32:25.
[21] See Colossians 3:5 and Ephesians 5:5.

The Faraway Idol

The faraway idol, which is a substitute for God's transcendence, is usually not very well defined. It is fashioned to give some overarching and ultimate meaning to life. Man, of course, was originally created to trust in God, but in his fallen condition, he creates a force or idea (an idol, if you will) that rules the universe in God's stead. When we listen, we can hear people saying that they believe there must be something, or someone, ultimately responsible for the way things are. Ask them what this is, and they are unable to describe him, her or it with any specificity. This, then, is the faraway idol.

Some say their god, because he is a loving god, could not send people to hell for an eternity. Again, this is a faraway idol, a construct that takes the place of the Sovereign of the universe who has said that He will, in fact, consign the disobedient to hell if they reject His gracious offer to save them through the blood of Jesus Christ. The true God is, of course, a God of love, as 1 John 4:8 makes clear, but the creator of this false god has made Love his faraway idol—the standard by which everything is to be judged.

A point of clarification needs to be made here. For the purpose of this study, I will continue to talk about the faraway idol, even though the faraway idol is not normally thought of by its adherents as an idol. This is because we normally think of an idol as something tangible, and the faraway idol is neither tangible nor visible. The following excerpt from the Roman author Cicero is an example of this kind of thinking:

> *When we behold the heavens, when we contemplate the celestial bodies, can we fail of conviction? Must we not acknowledge that there is a Divinity, a perfect being, a ruling intelligence, which governs, a God who is everywhere and directs all by his power?*

Anybody who doubts that may as well deny there is a sun that lights.... For this reason, with us as well as with other nations, the worship of the gods and holy exercises of religion increase in purity and extent every day.[22]

As we can see, the polytheism of Cicero's day embraced the faraway idol, which was a single transcendent "ruling intelligence," as well as the many nearby idols ("gods"), who were associated in the minds of their adherents with the different functions in the tangible, visible world. This clearly reflects the two levels of religious allegiances I've been discussing—the nearby idol, which is more accessible and which is directed toward power and control, and the faraway idol, which is far more inaccessible, but which provides meaning or legitimacy. Both of these (the faraway idol and the nearby idol) are representative of a universal trait that runs through all idolatry. And as idolatry is but the attempt to counterfeit the true God, it ought not to surprise us to hear Him asking His people in Jeremiah 23:23, "Am I a God near at hand...and not a God afar off?"

We can observe this faraway/nearby paradigm in the Canaanite pantheon. According to these people, "El the Benign," the Creator/Father/King, was the chief deity. As such, his mildly benevolent persona served, in the background, as the overarching presence in their religion. But even so, he was not thought to be nearly as effective in delivering concrete help as Baal, who was described in cult texts as one of the sons of Dagon, the national god of the Philistines. Baal became the Canaanites' fertility god, representing the powers of rain, fullness of life, and fertility. By the use of magic, incantations, rituals and priestcraft, they believed they

---

[22] From Charles Spurgeon, *The Treasury of David*, 1:279.

could exercise control over the forces of nature. Their worship of this nearby god was orgiastic and sensual, according to 1 Kings 14:22-24. Obviously, then, it was a religion enthusiastically pursued by its adherents. The Bible called the things these idolaters practiced "abominations," and those who practiced them "perverted persons." It was not just that Baal worship authorized sexual license, although this was a powerful incentive, but there was a much higher logic to it than this. The fertility gods and goddesses were thought to be voyeuristic. Consequently, it was believed that it was only through the sexual activity of humans that the fertility gods and goddesses were stimulated to lust after and pursue one another. Seduced by the human sexual activity they observed to engage in sexual intercourse themselves, they produced, it was believed, fertility on earth.

Paul's Mar's Hill Address

In his famous Mar's Hill address, delivered in the great city and seat of learning that was Athens, the apostle Paul systematically refuted the nearby and faraway idols with four alternating strokes, replacing them each time with the truth of God's transcendence and immanence. The points he makes, which are found in Acts 17, may be summarized as follows:

- First, he teaches that the one true God is not a faraway idol that is unknowable (verse 23).

- Then, he refutes their nearby idols by pointing out that God does not live in shrines made by human hands, nor does He need man's help in anything (verses 24-25).

- Next, he assaults the faraway idol by teaching the truth that God, although transcendent, is not far from any of us, for it is "In Him we live and move and have our being" (verses 27-28).

- Finally, he negates the nearby idol again by arguing that if we are truly God's offspring, then it makes absolutely no sense to think He can somehow derive His being from us. In other words, the one true God is not made of gold, silver or stone, and fashioned by human design (verse 29).

It seems clear that Paul directed his criticisms of the Athenians to the classic dual-nature of their idolatry. They had counterfeited the true God's transcendence with their faraway idol, "THE UNKNOWN GOD," and His immanence with the many nearby idols in their pantheon. With each criticism of their idolatry, Paul did not hesitate to make positive affirmations about the one true God. According to him, and this is consistent with everything else written in the Bible, the true God, although He is transcendent, is also very knowable (verse 23), in that He has revealed Himself to us in the holy Scriptures. Once he's made this point, he then proceeds to tell the Athenians about this one true God who is knowable. As the Creator, He is Lord of heaven and earth (verse 24). Consequently, He gives life to all people (verse 25). He made "From one blood" all nations that live on the earth, and He wants them to seek after, and find, Him (verses 26-27). Finally, He is, as the Creator, our source, in that we derive our existence from Him, not the other way around (verse 29).

As Paul argues, the one true God is, and all at the same time, both transcendent and immanent—i.e., He is both "far off" and "at hand."[23] In doing so, he conveys the ultimate moral challenge of this one true God, namely, "God...now commands all men

---

[23] See Jeremiah 23:23.

everywhere to repent" (verse 30). And why is this? Because He has appointed a day in which He will judge the world in righteousness by the Man whom He has ordained (verse 31). And who is this man? He is Jesus of Nazareth, in whom dwells "all the fullness of the Godhead bodily."[24] In fact, it is the incarnation of Jesus Christ that serves as the final blow to the dual-idolatry pattern that has plagued man down through the ages. The divine *Logos*, who was Himself the transcendent God of creation, according to John 1:1, became a man, as reported in John 1:14, the epitome of immanence, and did it all without ceasing to be God. In other words, "No one has ascended to heaven but He who came down from heaven, that is, the Son of Man who is in heaven."[25] The God of the Bible, the only true and living God, is a God who is "at hand," as well as "afar off."[26]

Unfortunately, and even though they ought to know better, some New Testament Christians fall victim to idolatry's dual pattern as they try to formulate their various Christologies. This is demonstrated in the classic heresies of Arianism, which denies the Lord's divine nature, and Docetism, which denies His human nature. By failing to appreciate the full meaning of the Immanuel (or "God with us") of Isaiah 7:14, both of these *isms* fall far short of the truth revealed in the Bible. Yes, and there must be no mistake about it, Jesus was a man, and His need for resurrection is proof of this. But, He was not just a man, as some among us are claiming, and His resurrection is proof of this, as well. If He were not a man, He could not have died and then been in need of resurrection. On the other hand, if He had not been "God manifested in the flesh,"

---

[24] Colossians 2:9.
[25] John 3:13.
[26] Jeremiah 23:23.

as He claimed to be in 1 Timothy 3:16, then the "one God and Father of all"[27] would certainly have not validated Jesus' claim by resurrecting Him from the dead.[28] Thus, any effort to separate the Lord's transcendence and immanence (i.e., His deity and humanity) will lead one down the path to self-sufficiency and idolatry.

The Jesus who is "a man, just a man, just an ordinary man like you and me" is an idol constructed by those among us who believe it may still be possible for a mere man to live perfectly and, therefore, earn his salvation. But such self-sufficiency is impossible, not because man does not have the capacity not to sin (viz., free will), he does; it's impossible because man wrongly exercises his free will. It is just here that some become confused, so please pay close attention as I say this once more. Man is a free will creature and, because he is, he does not have to sin. We are not made, contrary to Calvinistic doctrine, morally flawed or depraved. However, the rebellious story of mankind is that although we do not have to sin, we do—we always have and we always will.

The only man who ever lived perfectly here in this life was Jesus. Even so, He suffered and died. Why? Because, in His suffering and death, the Lord paid the penalty for the sins of all mankind. In doing so, He made it possible for all who had sinned, and this includes all of us, to be reconciled to God through obedience to Him. All of us—every last one of us—have sinned and fallen short of the glory of God.[29] So, when Jesus "died for all," it was because "all died."[30] This means that all human beings who reach the age of accountability will sin. It also means that even after being saved

---

[27] Ephesians 4:6.
[28] See Acts 17:31.
[29] See Romans 3:23.
[30] 2 Corinthians 5:14.

from our past sins by obedience to the gospel, Christians did not live perfectly without sin.[31] Consequently, the perfectionists among us who believe it is actually—as opposed to theoretically—possible for one to live without sinning, and have created a mere-man Jesus to prove it, teach a self-sufficiency that is anti-biblical and worship an idol that is both anti-God and "antichrist."[32] It is my sincere prayer that these false teachers will come to their senses in a pigsty moment,[33] repent, and adhere to John's warning to keep themselves from idols.[34]

As we can see, idolatry is still an ever present problem for New Testament Christians. We must not allow ourselves to be tricked into thinking that idolatry is a sin reserved just for pagans—it's not. Today, as in times past, the dark and dynamic forces behind idolatry[35] have arrayed themselves against us.[36] Drunk with the wine of modernity, many who make up the Lord's church in the 21st century believe the war is over and that it has actually been over for almost two thousand years now. This sort of thinking, as I hope to point out in the next section, has had devastating consequences for churches of Christ.

---

[31] See 1 John 1:10.
[32] 1 John 2:22.
[33] See Luke 15:17.
[34] See 1 John 5:21.
[35] See 1 Corinthians 10:20.
[36] See Ephesians 6:12.

Chapter 4

The Sham Gods Of "Orthotalksy"

For you shall worship no other god, for the LORD, whose name is Jealous, is a jealous God (Exodus 34:14).

No, it's not misspelled. "Orthotalksy" is a made-up word. It describes that which takes place when our concepts about God are wrong, but we continue to give lip-service to the "traditional," "correct," "accepted," or "orthodox" ways of talking about Him. For example, even though a brother erroneously comes to the conclusion that God is no longer actively involved in His creation, he will still give lip-service to being a firm believer in God's providence. Another brother, although he has concluded there are some things God simply cannot know, will, at the same time, continue to pay homage to His "all-knowingness." Yet another, while claiming to believe in the omnipotence of God, may teach that God's plan to redeem man through His Son, Jesus, could have failed. This is orthotalksy. Its immediate advantage is that it permits one to remain in the comfortable surroundings of "brotherhood soundness" while, at the same time, advocating new and radically false ideas about God.

According to *The American Heritage Dictionary*, "sham" means: "*1. Something false or empty that is purported to be genuine; a spurious imitation. 2. The quality of deceitfulness; empty pretense. 3. One who assumes a false character; an impostor.*" Therefore, a sham god is not God at all. All sham gods are idols and those who construct them are, quite simply, idolaters. This is true whether one is a pagan idolater involved in the construction of pagan images, or a brother involved in advancing the theological and philosophical concepts of modern-day theology.

There are other kinds of idolatry than those associated with the worship of pagan gods. A child of God who allows himself to get caught up in covetousness or greed is, according to the Bible, an idolater.[1] Further, in the first chapter of Romans, the apostle Paul makes it clear that changing "the glory of the incorruptible God into an image made like corruptible man" is idolatry. This is true whether it be an actual graven image or a theological construct.

This means that any one of us can be guilty of idolatry, and this is especially true of preachers. When one preaches, teaches, and writes about God and His Word, he must be willing to have what he says subjected to honest and fair criticism. Only a false teacher would object to this process. Of course, the standard for such criticism is not what I or anyone else might think. The spiritual benchmark for everything we believe and teach is the Bible—it alone is the objective standard.

Therefore, a religious discussion (or debate) should not be some frivolous academic exercise designed to entertain an audience. Nor is it designed to simply fill up space in some religious publication. It is, instead, a very serious undertaking designed to defend God and His word. Therefore, a debate, contrary to what some seem to think, is not a vehicle to showcase one's debating skills. The thing to be displayed in a religious debate should be either the truth or error of a particular position. If this is not the motive, then any such exercise would not be worth the time it takes to conduct it, or in the case of a written debate, the paper on which it is written.

When one undertakes to expound the attributes and characteristics of Almighty God, he is treading on hallowed ground. We

---

[1] See Colossians 3:5.

must approach any such undertaking with extreme reverence for the One we seek to clarify. Like Moses, we must take off our shoes, realizing we are standing on holy ground. A discussion/debate of God's word is the weightiest of matters.

To further impress us with the seriousness of these matters, the Bible, in James 3:1, makes it clear that the Bible teacher is under a stricter than normal judgment. Therefore, when we preach, teach, and write about God, we must do so carefully and reverently.

It is my firm belief that there is nothing more important than knowing the one true God! Our eternal destiny depends upon it.[2] Therefore, Bible teachers are involved in a most sobering endeavor. The task is to accurately communicate God and His Word. If, for whatever reason, we impose limits on the infinite God, we are engaged in idolatry. When we begin to think of God as a man, albeit a man of larger proportions, there ought to be no doubt that we are engaged in idolatry.

The God who has revealed Himself both in nature and the Scriptures is not a creature; that is, He is not a man.[3] He is not limited, as are His creatures, by anything outside of Himself. Consequently, He is nothing like the sham gods of paganism, nor the gelded God of modern theology.

In the following chapters, your attention will be directed to:

- The God Who Doesn't Do Anything,

- The God Who Doesn't Know The Future,

- The God Who Can Fail,

- The God Who Can Cease Being God,

---

[2] See John 17:3.
[3] See Numbers 23:19; 1 Samuel 15:29.

- The God Who Must Be Either Here Or There.

My intent is to expose these sham gods and the orthotalksy associated with them. In doing so, I will do my best to carefully, reverently and honorably defend the ontological integrity of Almighty God, Jehovah Elohim. Realizing that I am limited in my understanding of God's Word, I expect, and even invite, criticism. I assure you that all serious criticism will be taken to heart. If it can be shown from the Scriptures that I am wrong, in whole or in part, I would want my correction to be as public as my teaching. With this in mind, it is my prayer that God will bless us as we continue our study of this most critical of issues.

Chapter 5

The God Who Doesn't Do Anything

For in Him we live and move and have our being (Acts 17:28). And He is before all things, and in Him all things hold together (Colossians 1:17, ESV). Who [namely, Jesus] being the brightness of His glory and the express image of His person, and upholding all things by the word of His power (Hebrews 1:3).

Many of the pagan religions had a concept of a supreme creator-god, the one who brought the world into existence but, for one reason or another, was no longer actively involved in his creation. Even the Greek gods and goddesses who supposedly dwelt on Mt. Olympus were basically alienated from man and very rarely became involved with him. Aristotle's "Unmoved Mover" was totally uninterested in, and indifferent to, affairs on this earthly plane. Without thought of human affairs, Epicurus' gods dwelt in undisturbed bliss in the alleged void between the universes, eating, drinking and speaking Greek.

17th- and 18th-century Deism, although not classified as pagan, is the classic example of the world's inclination toward the idea of an absentee (or "faraway") God or gods. According to Deists, the Creator set the universe into motion and endowed it with everything necessary (i.e., "natural laws") for it to continue indefinitely. As such, our universe was thought to be the perfect perpetual motion machine. Since creation, the God of the Deists has not interfered with the natural laws He set in motion at the beginning. In his description of Deism, R. H. Tawney wrote: "...God has been thrust into the frigid altitudes of infinite space. There is a limited monarchy in heaven, as well as on earth. Providence was the spectator of the curious machine which it had constructed and set in motion, but the operation of which it was neither able nor willing to control..."[1]

Thomas "The Age of Reason" Paine, along with Thomas "Nature and Nature's God" Jefferson, and Benjamin "God helps those who help themselves" Franklin, to mention just three of our "Founding Fathers," fully imbibed the Deistic concept of God. Although religion was important to these men, it was, unfortunately, the rationalistic religion of nature. It was Paine who said, "My own mind is my church." Franklin went a step further and advocated a public religion that would promote good citizenship and morality, but would not meddle in affairs confined solely to the realm of reason (e.g., science and politics).

It seems clear that these ideas reflected the views of Voltaire, who said: "The only book that should be read is the great book of nature. The sole religion is to worship God and to be an honorable man. This pure and everlasting religion cannot possibly produce harm."[2] Thomas Jefferson's "Nature" and "Nature's God," mentioned in the *Declaration of Independence*, was, contrary to what some have thought, a reflection of Deist, not Christian, concepts—concepts which, once divorced from any idea of a Creator, would eventually develop into the secular humanism so prevalent in modern-day America.

The Deistic world view developed, in part, because of Newtonian physics, which at the time was a fairly new scientific theory.

---

[1] *The Acquisitive Society*, 1924, p. 13.
[2] From Andre Maurois' introduction to *Candide*, 1959, p. 6.

Newton's theory made it easy to think of the world as a great machine (viz., a clock) preset to run with amazing regularity. This new way of thinking played right into the hands of the Deists. In his description of Deism, Augustus H. Strong said, "God builds a house, shuts himself out, locks the door, and then ties his own hands in order to make sure of never using the key."[3]

What this meant was that, according to Deists, reason *alone* (i.e., reason unaided by special or supernatural revelation) would provide the ultimate solution to every problem. Unaided by any outside influence, man was the answer to his own problem, they thought. Eventually, this kind of thinking would come to be reflected in *Humanist Manifestos I and II*, which said, "No deity will save us; we must save ourselves."

This "clock-work" universe was a powerful influence in the development of American culture. Because we came to believe that nature is totally self-contained, we learned the necessity of being self-sufficient. As Americans who had, quite ironically, learned from our Puritan forefathers the necessity of hard work, we hunkered down and learned the lesson of self-sufficiency quite well. Supposing that the only two elements that keep the world going are natural law and human reason, we came to believe that "man can attack and overcome by education and technical means, and good will, all the evils of life."[4]

Understandably, Calvinism, the then prevalent "Christian" way of thinking, suffered immensely under this new world view. "The Calvinistic idea that man had absolutely nothing to do with

---

[3] *Systematic Theology*, 3 volumes in 1, 1907, p. 15.
[4] E. Graham Waring, editor, *Deism and Natural Religion*, p. xiii.

his own salvation made little sense to the frontiersman, who knew only too well that his temporal salvation was in his own hands."[5]

This new paradigm served us well. Realizing our own potential, and knowing our need to save ourselves, we pursued the improvement of our predicament with a passion that has yet to be surpassed. We improved our knowledge of our surroundings and discovered cures for diseases that had plagued mankind down through the centuries. Collectively and individually, we improved our lot. We invented machines that helped us grow in industrial might. Having conquered the work-a-day world, we then turned our attention to home and leisure and created gadgets that made life so much more comfortable than it had been before. Slowly, but surely, we developed into the masters of our own destiny. As such, we have become a nation of technological giants. Yes, there are those in other nations who make more money than we do, but no one actually lives better than Americans. But in the process of becoming technological giants, we evolved into a nation of moral and intellectual pygmies.

Today, hardly anyone wants to *think* and *know*. Instead, we desire to *feel* and *experience*. Therefore, that which reinforces our "feelings" about the rightness of our religion is not doctrine, which demands thinking, but sentiment, which only craves feelings. Even the goal of modern "Christianity" is not to change the hearer's mind, as much as it is to change his feelings. One such "sentiment" making the "Christian" circuit that aptly demonstrates this point is the idea that in order to heal emotionally we must first learn to forgive God for all the hurt we have experienced in our lives. Why? Because a God who is not omnipotent, like an

---

[5] William Warren Sweet, *Religion in the Development of American Culture: 1765-1840*, preface.

imperfect parent, ought to be forgiven for His shortcomings. From a biblical standpoint, such thinking is obviously wrong. But modern Christendom, which has thrown sound biblical doctrine overboard, no longer cares what people think about Bible doctrine. What it wants to know is how they feel: What do you *feel* is your problem? What do you *feel* should be the most important thing in your life? How do you *feel* about this, that and the other? Such has aptly been called "the religion of Dr. Feelgood," and there is no doubt that it is the religion of American Christendom.

This is the philosophical and theological environment in which we currently live. It appears that many of us who are members of Christ's church have not immunized ourselves from such. In fact, some of us have allowed such thinking to affect our minds. Having been taught that the age of miracles is over, some of us feel very comfortable with the materialistic rationalism now so prevalent in our society. Such comfortableness is a serious mistake that reflects a critical misunderstanding of God's Word. Yes, the Bible teaches that the miracles (i.e., "signs" and "wonders") that were so essential to the initial confirmation of God's Word[6] are no longer necessary.[7] Yes, the "perfect law of liberty"[8] has been "once for all delivered to the saints"[9] and, therefore, does not need to be continually confirmed or verified by miracles. However, and herein lies the crux of the matter, God, who is, by His very nature, supernatural, is still very much involved in this world.[10] Standing above and apart from our experiences (i.e., that which we can see, hear, touch, taste, and smell), there is a supernatural dynamic at work.

---

[6] See Mark 16:20; Hebrews 2:3-4.
[7] See 1 Corinthians 13:8-12.
[8] James 1:25.
[9] Jude 3.
[10] See Colossians 1:16-17; Hebrews 1:3.

The Christian & Idolatry

Unlike the sham gods of heathenism, Jehovah remains both interested and active in His creation.

Therefore, the idea of providence, the concept of a God who is active in His creation, is an important tenet of New Testament Christianity. In fact, the concept is so indigenous to a biblical world view that I have never known a Christian to actually deny it. What I have heard them do, however, is to describe God's providence in such a way as to, in essence, deny it. For example, I know of brethren who will *not* pray for the healing of those who have been classified as terminally ill. To do so, they think, would be asking God to perform a miracle, and God, they are quick to tell us, does not work that way today. When you ask these brethren if they believe in the providence of God, they say, "Of course!" What, then, do they mean when they say, "God's providence?" They mean, "God working in the natural world through natural means." This, of course, seems to be nothing more than Thomas Jefferson's "Nature" and "Nature's God." Therefore, when one of these brethren speaks of God's providence, while at the same time limiting this providence to nature, he is engaged in orthotalksy, whether he realizes it or not.

Teaching what the Bible says about the "chastening of the Lord"[11] meets with a great deal of resistance in many churches today. Why? "Because," we are told, "God simply does not work that way today." What way? "Well, you know, miracles; He no longer works miracles today." So? "Well, if He were actually in the business of chastening anyone today, He would be interjecting Himself into the world which, by definition, would be a supernatural act, something He has said in His Word that He would not be doing in this age." But where in His Word has God ever taught such a

---

[11] Hebrews 12:5.

doctrine? Unfortunately, it's about this time in the dialogue that someone usually begins to get upset.

In Hebrews 12:5-8, the Scriptures say:

My son, do not despise the chastening of the Lord, nor be discouraged when you are rebuked by Him; for whom the Lord loves He chastens, and scourges every son whom He receives. If you endure chastening, God deals with you as with sons; for what son is there whom a father does not chasten? But if you are without chastening, of which all have become partakers, then you are illegitimate and not sons.

In other words, the Bible teaches that the Lord is actively involved in disciplining His children. How He does this I cannot be sure, but there is nothing in the Bible that teaches me that it must be done "only in and through the Word," as many seem to think. Furthermore, anyone who gives lip-service to God's providence—in this case, special providence—but denies He is involved in the chastening of His sons, is engaged in orthotalksy.

After doing some writing on the activity of Satan and his demonic horde, a preacher contacted me about what he thought to be problems with what I had written. His position, which has been widely read in the brotherhood, is that Satan, since his defeat by Jesus Christ, is locked away in prison and has no immediate input into the struggle currently taking place between the kingdom of light and the kingdom of darkness. Satan's only influence on the world, according to this brother, is residual. His agents are not demons, but men and women who have been influenced to do evil by the false teachings that have filtered down through the ages. According to this brother, the "doctrines of demons," that some were going to fall prey to in the "latter times,"[12] were not doctrines taught *by* demons; they were, instead, false doctrines *about* demons, who were, in reality, nothing more than the figments of man's imagination.

Although it is true that Satan has been defeated by our Lord and is, consequently, limited in what he can do, he is still very much a part of the battle raging here on planet Earth. The Bible makes it clear that this defeated enemy is still a formidable foe who goes about, according to 1 Peter 5:8, as a roaring lion, seeking whom he may devour. In other words, the Bible identifies Satan as the "Lame-Duck" ruler of this world who remains active (although curtailed) between the "D-Day" of the cross and the "V-Day" of the Lord's Second Coming. When I asked my brother about this verse, he said it was just a metaphor and was not meant to be taken literally. Acknowledging that the passage was speaking of the Devil metaphorically, I asked him if he thought the metaphor accurately depicted his position that Satan is locked away in a prison somewhere and is unable to have any direct influence on the world in which we live. In reply, he just repeated that the passage was a metaphor and not to be taken literally. To me, it sounded like this brother was saying 1 Peter 5:8 is no longer valid.

In contrast to the idea that Satan is no longer active, the Bible teaches that we must guard our minds against Satan's onslaughts. It teaches that the Devil can both blind[13] and corrupt our minds through deception.[14] In opposition to the wisdom that comes from above, we are told there is the wisdom that comes from below—a

---

[12] 1 Timothy 4:1.
[13] See 2 Corinthians 4:4.
[14] See 2 Corinthians 11:3.

wisdom that is earthly, sensual, and devilish.[15] Those exhibiting this kind of wisdom, according to Ephesians 2:2-3, are "walking according to the prince of this world." So, even when I grant that the immediate cause of much of this is residual, as my esteemed brother correctly teaches, this in no way prevents Satan from being directly (personally) or indirectly (through his angels, demons, evil spirits or human agents) involved in deluding and blinding mankind to the Truth. And although it is absolutely true that none of this can happen without our cooperation, it does, in fact, happen. How do I know? The Bible tells me so.

But this is not all. The Bible teaches that if we do not love the truth, God will permit us to be deluded.[16] The one who has God's permission to do this deluding is the "the prince of the power of the air, the spirit who now works in the sons of disobedience."[17] Therefore, we are instructed to put on the "whole armor of God" so that we will be able to stand against "all the wiles" of the Devil.[18] Incidentally, the very context of Ephesians 6 is, "For we do not wrestle against flesh and blood, but against principalities, against powers, against the rulers of the darkness of this age, against spiritual hosts of wickedness in the heavenly places" (v. 12). This is not just theological fiddle-faddle, as some seem to think. This is, instead, the clear and emphatic teaching of God's Word. This is why the Scriptures instruct us to "gird up the loins of [our] mind[s]."[19] Unfortunately, too many of us think and act like there is no real battle going on today. But make no mistake about it, there is a real

---

[15] See James 3:15.
[16] See 2 Thessalonians 2:7-12.
[17] Ephesians 2:2.
[18] Ephesians 6:11.
[19] 1 Peter 1:13.

battle going on in our time, and the object of this battle is our minds.

When I asked my brother why the Holy Spirit would have spent so much time warning us about something that could not, according to his belief, happen anyway, he insisted, quite emphatically, that Satan was not able to put ideas into our minds today. When I asked, Why not?, he first argued that it would be a violation of our free wills. So, I pointed out to him that Satan put something into the mind of Judas without violating his free will.[20] He then argued that if Satan were permitted to do this today, then he would be exercising more power than God. How was this?, I asked. "Well," he said, "God works only in and through the Word today, and if Satan can put things into our minds, then he is exercising more power than God."[21]

I assured my brother that although I understood the Bible to be teaching that no one can be saved apart from his obedience to the gospel, I do not believe it teaches that God is limited to working "only in and through the Word," whether it be in conversion, or anywhere else. "Well," he said, "name something God does today apart from His Word." I then spent a few moments trying to assure him that I did not want to denigrate the Word of God in any sense. Nevertheless, I told him, I believe there is nothing in the Bible that teaches that God's providence (whether general or special) must take place "only in and through the Word." In conjunction with this, I pointed out that if wisdom came "only in and through the Word," then the command in James 1:5-7 is grossly misleading. In this passage, we are asked to pray for wisdom, which the Lord will

---

[20] See John 13:2.
[21] Although this quote may not be word for word, it accurately represents the essence of what this brother said.

then give to those who ask in faith. Contextually, this wisdom is not limited to a study of God's Word which, I pointed out, does provide wisdom, but encompasses that which is received directly from God in response to our prayers. But according to my brother, this is simply not so. He contended, unflinchingly, that because we no longer live in the miraculous age, God has *limited* His actions to the Word. Therefore, he argued if Satan could directly influence our minds today, then he would definitely be more powerful than God. The conclusion of the matter, as far as the aforementioned brother is concerned, is that God is limited to working "only in and through the Word" today. Any other conclusion, he believes, leads us into the deluded fallacies of Pentecostalism.

Brethren, the Scriptures teach that we are engaged in a great spiritual battle against a mighty host of spiritual wickedness. That there are more than a few among us who do not understand this is indicative of the degree to which we have absorbed the spirit of this age. It seems that some of us have become 21st century Sadducees, believing neither in angels nor spirits,[22] and "knowing neither the Scriptures nor the power of God."[23]

Yes, Pentecostalism is certainly filled to the brim with "deluded fallacies." But as wrong as Pentecostalism is, at least Pentecostals believe in a God who is still actively involved in His creation. That so many of God's people no longer believe that He is, is, in my opinion, a grievous error that plagues the modern church, and reflects the teachings of the modified neo-Deists who stand in our pulpits today and preach both an absentee God and a watered down Gospel.

---

[22] cf. Acts 23:8.
[23] Matthew 22:29.

Some, no doubt, will be terribly troubled by what I'm saying. Others will detect in what I have written an "uncouth and impertinent stridency." In fact, one dear brother, who I greatly respect for his work's sake, said I sounded like I had a chip on my shoulder. Well, he may be right, but I think he may be wrong about just what that "chip" is. I plead guilty to feeling under tremendous pressure concerning these things. I attribute this to a zeal for the Lord's house,[24] a reverent fear of "He Who Is,"[25] and a genuine love of the Truth.[26] Of course, I pray that I am right about this. If I know my own heart, and I know the heart can be a terribly deceptive place, I am not trying to "get even" with anyone. As I have already said, I believe preaching to be valuable work. Therefore, I am not anti-preacher or anti-preaching. Nevertheless, I am convinced that many Christians today wrongly believe what they believe, not because they have learned it from the Bible, but because they have learned it by listening to the modified neo-Deists in our pulpits. Let me be frank. At issue is not whether the things I am saying are deemed by some to be rude and discordant—at issue is this: Is what I am saying true?

When a knowledgeable Buddhist is first introduced to Christianity, the first thing that would strike him as novel about Jehovah is *not* that He is a God of love or that He is a God of self-sacrifice. Instead, he would be struck with the idea that Jehovah is a God who *actively participates* in the world. As was previously pointed out, many religions and classic philosophies picture a God who is absent from the world rather than active in it. But this is not so when it comes to the God who has revealed Himself

---

[24] See John 2:17.
[25] Proverbs 9:10; Isaiah 8:13.
[26] See 2 Thessalonians 2:10.

in the Bible. As Jesus said in John 5:17, "My Father has been working until now." That is, there never has been a time when God was not actively involved in His creation.

Unfortunately, many Christians believe, along with the Deists, that God created the universe, set the natural laws in motion, and now sits back and lets the whole thing run on its own. In fairness to these Christians, and in contrast to the Deists, it ought to be pointed out that they believe the Lord has, on various occasions, interjected Himself into His creation. In other words, they believe the Creator has from time to time acted in, and upon, His creation. Primarily, they believe this participation was for the express purpose of effecting man's redemption. Therefore, they do not believe that God cannot be active in His creation. Instead, they believe that Jehovah is not, by His own choice, at this time, actively involved in the world. I believe I know how and why they have come to these conclusions. I am even sympathetic. Even so, I do not think their conclusions are consistent with the truths taught in the Bible.[27]

The scope of this study does not permit us to enter into a detailed study of the providence of God, or as I now prefer to call it, "the hand of God."[28] Nevertheless, the nature of this study compels me to mention some things. I do not, for instance, deny the reality of what we call the "laws of nature." These laws (e.g., gravity, motion, physics, chemistry, and thermodynamics) are well-established and very much a part of our ordered universe. It seems to me that the actual existence of these laws cannot be intelligently

---

[27] Anyone who has kept up with the wranglings between Old Earth and Young Earth creationists in recent years should now understand why so many Christians are getting caught up in Old Earth creationism, which is not much more than modified neo-Deism.
[28] 1 Peter 5:6.

denied. But, when we speak of these laws of nature, are we talking about purely descriptive devices, or are we talking about things that actually explain why things happen? In other words, do the natural laws only describe the way things happen or do they actually explain why things happen the way they do? I believe a correct understanding of natural laws must combine both of these concepts. The next question ought to be: Why should there be such laws in the first place? All of us, I am sure, answer this question the same way: Because God created them! Yes, this is certainly true, and even a Deist could answer this way, but the crucial question is: Is there more to this? I answer by saying, yes, there is, and it is at this point that I begin to part company with my modified neo-Deist brethren.

The Bible teaches that not only did God create the natural laws, and then set them in motion, but He also keeps them in motion.[29] This means that God's work with reference to the natural laws was not over when He finished creating the universe. Even now, He continues to uphold all things by the "word of His power."[30] That is to say, "In Him all things consist," or "hold together."[31]

This means that "in Him" the atomic particles cling to their positions around their nuclei. It means that "in Him" molecules cohere to form elements. "In Him" the elements form various substances and bodies. "In Him" the gravitational pull of the earth causes us to stick to its surface. "In Him" the planets revolve around the sun. "In Him" our galaxy holds together as a clump of stars rushing with great speed through the massive expanse of the universe. And what does all this mean? It means that God

---

[29] See Acts 17:28; Colossians 1:17; Hebrews 1:3.
[30] Hebrews 1:3.
[31] Colossians 1:17.

continues to preserve the whole universe, preventing it from slipping back into nonexistence or nothingness. It means that even the most fundamental physical law of the universe, the first law of thermodynamics (i.e., the law of energy conservation), remains in force as a direct result of God's providence. This means the creation is totally and continuously dependent upon the power of God for its existence (i.e., "in Him we live, and move, and have our being").[32]

Finally, although Jehovah must never be thought of as the theologian's "god of the gaps," it just may be that the quirkiness that seems to be taking place on the subatomic level (we're talking quantum physics here), namely, "effects without causes," is nothing other than the "hand of God" supernaturally holding all things together by "the word of His power." I am not saying it *is*, mind you. What I am saying is that it *could be*. It is certainly not inconsistent with what the Bible teaches concerning God's providential care.[33]

In concluding this part of our study, let me restate my position as succinctly as I know how. The God of the Bible is not an absentee God. He is not uninvolved in His creation. He is now, has been in the past, and will continue to be in the future, actively "upholding all things by the word of His power." While He has bestowed a degree of autonomy upon His creation, even providing the crowning glory of His creation with free moral agency, He, nevertheless, reserves for Himself the final decision as to whether a particular

---

[32] Acts 17:28a.

[33] The fact that Colossians 1:17 and Hebrews 1:3 specifically mention God the Son should not be interpreted to mean that the Father and Holy Spirit are no longer involved in the work of providence. On the contrary, these passages simply include the Son in this work and, thereby, serve to affirm His true identity as God.

event occurs or not. Because "He is who He is,"[34] Jehovah can allow something to happen in association with His natural laws, or He can intervene to prevent it. By manipulating, limiting, or even overriding these laws, He can cause another event—one that would not have "normally" taken place—to occur instead.

On certain occasions, and for His own purposes, God has even granted this ability to Satan.[35] Among other things, Satan, with God's permission, caused the great wind that destroyed Job's family. In Job 2:7, this arch enemy of all mankind is identified as the one who "smote" Job. What does all this mean? The ramifications reach far beyond the scope of this study. But of this one thing I am certain: God is the absolute Sovereign—i.e., Ruler, King, Authority—over all creation.[36] As Sovereign, He retains the right to intervene in and overrule any, or all, of His natural laws.

According to 2 Peter 3:10-13, that which was brought into existence and is currently maintained by the "word of His power" shall be demolished by God. It is only the Eternal One, the One who was, is, and shall be, who has the capacity to be the Creator, Sustainer, *and* Destroyer of the universe. In all eternity, only He is present. Accordingly, the one and only true God in no way resembles the absentee, do-nothing gods of either heathenism or modern theology. The idea that the laws of nature are so "fixed" as to leave no room for divine intervention is completely foreign to the pages of the Bible. Therefore, when a Christian claims to believe in the providence of God, but then limits this providence to the natural processes alone, he is genuflecting to the sham gods of orthotalksy.

---

[34] Exodus 3:14.
[35] See Job 1:12-19.
[36] See Daniel 4:32-34; 5:21; Psalm 103:19; 145:1-21; Ephesians 1:20-22; Jude 25.

Chapter 6

The God Who Doesn't Know The Future

Him being delivered by the determined counsel and foreknowledge of God, you have taken by lawless hands, having crucified, and put to death (Acts 2:23). Elect according to the foreknowledge of God the Father (1 Peter 1:2).

The world is filled with the sham gods of religion, science, and philosophy. Alfred North Whitehead (1861-1947), the son of an Anglican vicar, and a professor at both Cambridge and Harvard, was well-known for his work in the philosophy of science and mathematics, and eventually became the systematizer of a way of thinking that has come to be known as "Process philosophy." This philosophy, also known as Panentheism, teaches that God, who is both relative and mutable, grows or develops along with His creation. This philosophy eventually evolved into what is today known as "Process theology" which, according to its proponents, is "the most important development in Christian thought since the first century."[1] The reason this movement is so popular today is that it provides us sophisticated moderns with an intellectually and emotionally satisfying reinterpretation of Christianity that seems to be in complete

---

[1] Ronald Nash, ed., *Process Theology*, 1987, in the Introduction.

agreement with so many of the ways of thinking that became acceptable in the latter half of the twentieth century.

Chief among Whitehead's followers is Charles Hartshorne, who summarized his dissatisfaction with classical theism in a book entitled *Omnipotence and Other Theological Mistakes*. In addition to the idea of omnipotence, he singled out the "mistakes" of God's perfection, omniscience, love, and immutability. Hartshorne thinks Greek and Roman philosophy has had too much influence on classical theism. His desire, therefore, is to rid us of these encumbrances and replace them with a truly enlightened and modern view of biblical faith. As we observe the changes some of our own brethren are making in their reinterpretations of God's characteristics and attributes, it is relevant to note that Hartshorne affirms divine omniscience, but then redefines it in a radically different way than we normally think of the word. Omniscience, according to Hartshorne, is the ability to "know all that exists." But because future, contingent, free will choices have not happened yet, they do not exist, and if they do not exist, they cannot be known even by an omniscient God. Hartshorne calls this "temporal omniscience." This is exactly the idea that some brethren are currently defending. I have suspected for some time that the various concepts some of my brethren are defending and teaching reflect a study of Process philosophy more than they do the Word of God. If I am right, this will become more obvious as time goes on.

Process theology, according to those who have critiqued it, is a total capitulation to paganism. "Take any essential Christian belief," these critics say, "and one will find that the process theologians supplant it with an alien belief."[2] Is God the Sovereign of the universe? Is He the personal, omnipotent, and all-knowing

---

[2] *Ibid.*

Creator of the universe? Is Jesus Christ the eternal, divine Son of God whose incarnation, death, and resurrection were necessary in order to redeem fallen man? Is faith in Christ the only foundation for human forgiveness? To these, and many other questions, the official Process answer is "No."

Just how many of our brethren have read after Whitehead and Hartshorne, I have no way of knowing. But this is what I do know. The books of those who have been influenced by Whitehead, Hartshorne, *et al.*, have found their way into the libraries of our brethren. One example would be *God's Foreknowledge and Man's Free Will*. The author of this book, Richard Rice, believes that God's knowledge is "constantly increasing."[3] According to Rice, God does not have *actual* foreknowledge of the future, contingent, free will choices of men and women. He teaches that God's prophetic utterances are nothing more than predictions based upon His perfect knowledge of the past and infinite knowledge of the present, or His omnipotence, which He uses to make things happen, or a combination of both of these.[4] It has not gone unnoticed that Rice's book is being recommended by some brethren as the definitive answer to the question associated with the alleged "incompatibleness of God's foreknowledge and man's free will." I'll have more to say about this further along in this study, but now I want to address the idea of God's all-knowingness.

Psalm 147:5 says that God's knowledge is infinite. Infinite in this verse is the Hebrew *micpar* and means the same thing it does in English. Now, if God's understanding is infinite (i.e., having no boundaries or limits), and understanding is predicated on knowledge, then it follows necessarily that God's knowledge is also

---

[3] 1985, pages 30, 39.
[4] Rice, pages 75ff.

infinite. Of course, such infinite knowledge would, in fact, be "unsearchable" by finite creatures, and this is exactly what Romans 11:33 says. In other words, God "knows all things."[5] Notice that the Bible does not say God has the *capacity* to know all things, which He certainly does; instead, the argument is that God *actually* "knows all things." Now, if God knows all things, what is it that He does not know? Remember, the Great Intelligence of the universe is writing to His intelligent creatures and expects us to be able to understand what He's saying. Accordingly, not only does He teach us through direct statements and approved examples, but He also expects us to make necessary conclusions. So, by direct statement the Bible teaches that God "knows all things," and the necessary conclusion is that there is not anything God does not know—and this includes the *then*, *now*, and *not yet*!

This seems plain enough. The Bible teaches in no uncertain terms that there is not anything God does not know. This includes even those things that modern science tells us cannot be known. For example, in quantum physics there is an axiom known as *Heisenberg's indeterminacy principle* which says that one cannot know the exact position and the exact speed of any atomic particle at the same time. This means that if we calculate the speed of an electron, we cannot know its position. On the other hand, if we calculate the electron's position, then we cannot know its speed. To do both is a practical and theoretical impossibility. Even so, what is quite impossible for man to discern is clearly known by God. In fact, God does not just know the location and speed of a particular atomic particle, He actually knows the position and speed of all atomic particles that make up the universe.

---

[5] 1 John 3:20.

Again, the Bible teaches in no uncertain terms that there is not anything God does not know. But some say that this is not true. As has been previously mentioned, there are those who believe there are some things God just cannot know, particularly the future, contingent, free will choices of men and women. On the other hand, there are those who believe that God has the capacity to know all things but, for reasons known only to Him, chooses not to know some of these things. This, I think, is pretty much the orthodox view within churches of Christ. Unlike those previously mentioned, who advocate their position primarily for philosophical reasons, those who advocate this position do so only because the Bible seems to be saying that there are things God did not know[6] and, as they are accustomed to saying, the Bible does not contradict itself. I shall be answering the questions presented by both of these arguments, but I will answer the latter group first.

True, the Bible does not contradict itself. Therefore, if the Bible teaches that there is not anything God does not know, then passages like Genesis 18 and 22—which are the proof-texts of those who believe God does not know some things—must be interpreted in light of this truth. In fact, a fundamental rule of Bible interpretation says that we must understand Scripture in its normal sense unless a literal interpretation contradicts other clear teaching found in God's Word. This is the error one makes in thinking Genesis 18 and 22 negate the all-knowingness of God. Nevertheless, it is argued by these brethren that just as God being all-powerful does not mean He has to be doing everything He has the capacity to do, neither does being all-knowing mean God must know everything He has the capacity to know. What to many sounds like incontestable logic is, in fact, a *non sequitur*, that is to say, an argument that does

---

[6] See Genesis 18:21 and 22:12.

not logically follow its premise. True, being all-powerful, by definition, does not mean one has to be engaged in doing all things; but knowing all things, by definition, does mean "knowing all things." Being all-powerful infers ability only, while being all-knowing infers not just ability, but the actual knowledge itself. In other words, the God of the Bible is not claiming that He *could* know all things; He's claiming He *does* know all things.

Those who wrongly believe Genesis 18 and 22 to be teaching that God has chosen not to know some things ignore the plain teaching of these scriptures by their literal interpretation of these passages. Of course, fairness compels me to admit that it is equally possible for one to argue that I am doing the same thing. My task, therefore, is to demonstrate the actual accord that exists between two seemingly contradictory teachings—(1) God knows all things; (2) God does not know some things—and do it in a way that does no damage to the integrity of the Scriptures. What follows is my explanation of what appears, at first, to be a dilemma.

In Genesis 18:21, we are dealing with an unusual circumstance. God, who is omnipresent, which means His ontological being is present to all of space equally, has, on occasion, entered space at specific points and become present in it for a specific purpose. The theologians call these "theophanies." This seems to be the case in Genesis 18:21. In verse 1 of the chapter, it says, "Then the LORD appeared to him [Abraham] by the terebinth trees of Mamre, as he was sitting in the tent door in the heat of the day." In verse 2, it mentions "three men." Whether these three men are manifestations of the triune nature of God, or whether the other two were angels, is not clear. What seems clear is that this is, in fact, a theophany. In entering the time-space continuum, God, who is infinite ontologically, willingly, and somehow, without ceasing to be who He is, allowed Himself to be subject to the finite. It's mind-boggling, I know, but, nevertheless, this appears to be the clear import of Scripture. Now, let's look at Genesis 18:21 with my interpretation of it in parentheses:

> *I, [who have somehow subjected Myself to the time-space continuum] will go down [not from heaven, but down the way geographically]* **now** *[not in eternity, but right now at this moment, subject to time and space] and see [i.e., learn experientially in time and space] whether they have done [and, more importantly, continue to do "now"] altogether according to the outcry against it that has come to Me [in eternity, not limited by time and space]; and if not [i.e., if they are no longer doing what I knew they were doing before I allowed Myself to be subject to time and space], I [God subject to time and space] will know [experientially].*

Notice that I have emphasized the word "now" by putting it in bold letters. This is because I believe this word to be the key to understanding this passage. God, who ontologically knows the past, present, and future, contextualizes His knowing to the "now" of the time-space continuum. Are we really supposed to think that the self-existent, eternal, infinite Spirit who is God did not really know everything that had been happening in Sodom and Gomorrah? 1 John 3:20 makes it absolutely clear that God is greater than our heart (He knows our heart as well as every other heart) and knows all things. No, whatever Genesis 18:21 means must be understood by the context, and the context clearly indicates a theophany. Therefore, the theophany must be taken into consideration when trying to understand this passage. When I debated the brother in the Foreknowledge of God debate mentioned in chapter one, he did take the position that God cannot know the future. But even so, he at least admitted that God knew the past and present perfectly. His position was bad enough, I think, but now some are wanting me to believe that the all-knowing God does not even know the past and present perfectly. True, this is the *only conclusion* one may come to if this passage is to be understood literally and apart from its "now" context. Therefore, I know *this conclusion* is not, and cannot be, true!

I now ask you to turn your attention to what I consider the more difficult passage. In Genesis 22:12, the angel of the Lord says to Abraham, "Do not lay your hand on the lad, or do anything to him; for **now** I know that you fear God, since you have not withheld your son, your only son, from Me." Although the "angel of the Lord" is involved in this episode, the unusual circumstances associated with a theophany are not a part of the context. Furthermore, as we have already observed, the Bible teaches us that the self-existent, eternal, and infinite Spirit who is God "knows all things." So, again, citing a fundamental principle of hermeneutics, this passage cannot be interpreted in a way that would negate this truth.

Now, in connection with all this, it is interesting to note *what* the self-existent, eternal, infinite Spirit who is God knew about Abraham before He ever "tested" him. In Genesis 18:17-19, the Lord said:

> *Shall I hide from Abraham what I am doing, since Abraham shall surely become a great and mighty nation, and all the nations of the earth shall be blessed in him? For I have known him, in order that he may command his children and his household after him, that they keep the way of the Lord, to do righteousness and justice, that the Lord may bring to Abraham what He has spoken to him.*

In other words, God knew that Abraham would pass the "tests" of faith, which included the one mentioned in this passage. To disregard this information, as well as the truth about God's "all-knowingness," is to make a serious mistake when trying to understand this passage. Yes, taken literally, the passage does appear to be teaching that God learned something about Abraham that He had not previously known. But, if God really does know all things, and the Bible says He does, and if He knew Abraham would pass all "tests," and the Bible says He did, then Genesis 22:12 cannot be teaching what it seems to be teaching.[7]

I think the answer to understanding Genesis 22:12 is found in places like Deuteronomy 29 and 30, where God promises to give life or death and blessings or cursings, depending upon one's obedience to His Word. Do what is right and one is blessed; do what is wrong and one is cursed. This is, in fact, a principle taught many places in the Bible. Although we do not expect to hear the voice of the "angel of the Lord" today, nevertheless, this principle is still true: If we serve the Lord faithfully, He will bless us; if we disobey Him, He will curse us.

God is all-knowing. This is what the Bible clearly teaches. This means that He has infallible remembrance of the past, infinite consciousness of the present, and complete foreknowledge of the future. Even so, He has agreed to deal with us in the time-space continuum. In the passage cited, you will notice that I have once again emphasized the word "now." This is because I believe the key to understanding this passage, like the key to understanding

---

[7] I admit to feeling a little uncomfortable when making this kind of statement. Nevertheless, I am confident that this is the correct way to think about this passage. The apostle Paul was not the only inspired writer who wrote things difficult to understand, which, if we are not careful, can be twisted to teach something completely contrary to truth (cf. 2 Peter 3:16). Our responsibility is to be diligent to present ourselves approved to God, as workers who do not need to be ashamed, rightly dividing the word of truth (2 Timothy 2:15). This is not always easy, but if we work hard at it, then we, like Abraham, will also pass the "test."

Genesis 18:21, is the "now" context. In the "now" of Abraham's time and space, the voice of the angel of the Lord could be heard audibly, and God is acknowledging His blessing on, or appreciation of, Abraham at a very critical time and place in his "walk of faith." It should not go unnoticed that the word "know" in this passage is sometimes translated "to recognize, admit, acknowledge, confess, declare, or tell." So, in harmony with the rest of Scripture, and without doing any violence to the words of this passage, Genesis 22:12 is not teaching that the all-knowing God of the universe did not really know whether Abraham would pass this critical test. Instead, He is acknowledging His appreciation of Abraham's faithfulness to Him. In other words, He is declaring, "Abraham, I have been testing you...and you have passed the test!"

This question seems to bother many Christians. How, they wonder, can God treat us like we are saved **now**, if He really knows we are going to be lost later? This kind of thinking, of course, projects onto God our own human incapabilities. Again, we need to be reminded that God is "not a man"[8] and, as such, is not subject to human limitations. If we all really believed this, then this problem would never arise in the minds of some. Whether these folks are consciously aware of it or not, they have conceived in their minds a sham god who suffers from finite limitations while hypocritically verbalizing their faith in the omni-characteristics of Almighty God. Hence, the god these people worship is pagan, and the language they speak is orthotalksy.

The God of the Bible has agreed to deal with us exactly where we are in the time-space continuum—namely, if we do what is right, He blesses us; but if we do what is wrong, He curses us. As was pointed out in the previous section, this principle is taught

---

[8] See Numbers 23:19; 1 Samuel 15:29.

many places in God's Word. This means that God does repent and He does relent as He deals with His free moral agents.[9] When one obeys the gospel and is added to the church by Christ Himself, he has been saved from his past sins[10] and has access to the spiritual blessings available only "in Christ."[11] As such, he or she is adopted by God as His own child, with all the privileges associated with such status.[12] Even if this individual will eventually fall from grace[13] and have his or her name removed from the Book of Life,[14] God can, and does, deal with this person in a perfectly righteous way. What one will eventually do, or not do, does not prohibit God from interacting with His creatures exactly the way He said He would. Surely, one ought to be willing to listen to God's own testimony on this. In Jeremiah 42, God set forth two options for the people: (1) Do what is right and I will bless you (verses 10-12); (2) Do what is wrong and I will curse you (verses 13-18). In Ezekiel 33:11-19, the Lord said:

> *Say to them: 'As I live,' says the Lord GOD, 'I have no pleasure in the death of the wicked, but that the wicked turn from his way and live. Turn, turn from your evil ways! For why should you die, O house of Israel? Therefore you, O son of man, say to the children of your people: The righteousness of the righteous man shall not deliver him in the day of his transgression; as for the*

---

[9] It must be understood that this "repenting" and "relenting" on God's part has nothing to do with His specific irrevocable decisions—decisions in which any amount of intercession on man's part or repentance on God's part will change (cf. Ezekiel 24:13-14).
[10] See Acts 2:47.
[11] Ephesians 1:3.
[12] See Romans 8:14-17.
[13] See Galatians 5:4.
[14] See Revelation 3:5;22:19.

wickedness of the wicked, he shall not fall because of it in the day that he turns from his wickedness; nor shall the righteous be able to live because of his righteousness in the day that he sins. When I say to the righteous that he shall surely live, but he trusts in his own righteousness and commits iniquity, none of his righteous works shall be remembered; but because of the iniquity that he has committed, he shall die. Again, when I say to the wicked, 'You shall surely die,' if he turns from his sin and does what is lawful and right, if the wicked restores the pledge, gives back what he has stolen, and walks in the statutes of life without committing iniquity, he shall surely live; he shall not die. None of his sins which he has committed shall be remembered against him; he has done what is lawful and right; he shall surely live. Yet the children of your people say, 'The way of the LORD is not fair.' But it is their way which is not fair! When the righteous turns from his righteousness and commits iniquity, he shall die because of it. But when the wicked turns from his wickedness and does what is lawful and right, he shall live because of it.

This, then, is what God has agreed to do, and through faith we can be sure He does it. Doubt this, and we doubt the God who has revealed Himself in Scripture.

Before leaving this section, we need to look at one more point. God knew that Judas would betray His Son.[15] Jesus knew that Judas would betray Him.[16] All this was before Judas acted to betray Jesus. Is there anything in Scripture that indicates this knowledge caused our Lord to treat Judas any differently than He would have if Judas was not going to be the one who would betray Him? In other words, did Jesus behave unfairly with Judas or mistreat him

---

[15] See Psalm 41:9; Acts 2:23.
[16] See John 6:70-71.

in any way? Of course not! Now, if God could deal fairly with Judas, who would betray His only begotten Son, then there should be no doubt that He can deal fairly with us in the time-space continuum. If we do what is right, we can be sure He will bless us. On the other hand, if we do evil, we can be certain He will curse us.

There are those among us who believe that God's foreknowledge and man's free will are incompatible. They believe this incompatibility is "axiomatic," or self-evident, truth. Consequently, they feel compelled to make a choice between God's foreknowledge or man's free will. Wishing to preserve the biblical concept of man's free moral agency, they conclude that God does not have foreknowledge of man's future, contingent, free will acts. These brethren are making a serious mistake—a mistake that has caused them to erect a sham god who cannot know the future. When expounding their position, these brethren immerse themselves in the shibboleths of orthotalksy.

Contrary to what these brethren think, the Bible teaches that God has foreknowledge of man's future, contingent, free will acts. For example, just before he died, Moses was told by God of the coming apostasy of the Israelites.[17] God was not just declaring what He planned to do, but was making it clear what human beings would be doing in the future of their own free wills. In addition, the Bible teaches that man has free will.[18] Therefore, the Bible teaches both God's foreknowledge of the future, contingent, free will choices of His creatures and man's free will.

Furthermore, it is not true that God's foreknowledge and man's free will are irreconcilable. This is the figment of some philosopher's imagination. Unfortunately, John Calvin fell victim to

---

[17] See Deuteronomy 31:16-21.
[18] In places like Deuteronomy 30:19, *et cetera*.

this thinking and instead of opting for man's free will, he chose to believe in God's foreknowledge. According to Calvin, man just does not have free will. Today, Calvinism is one of the most prevalent false doctrines in Christendom. Calvin's God knows all that is going to happen in the future because He is the one who has decreed everything that will happen. According to this false doctrine, man simply does what God has decided He will do. Some, we are told, have been predestined for heaven; others have been predestined for hell. All of this, according to Calvin, was completely independent of any decision on man's part. This, in a nutshell, is the soul of Calvinism. The entire theological system, of course, is quite detailed and very complicated. It may surprise some to learn that it is also very logical. But this is true only if one accepts Calvin's starting premise—namely, it is axiomatic that God's foreknowledge and man's free will are totally inconsistent.

Parenthetically, I have always considered it ironic, and perhaps even a little cynical, that brethren who disagree with me concerning my teaching that God's omniscience includes the sum total of things past, present, and future have always felt the necessity to warn me about what they think are my Calvinistic predispositions, and all this while they, themselves, are advancing Calvin's major premise. What am I talking about? Well, look at it. Brethren who believe God either *chooses* not to know some things or *cannot* know some things take these positions in order to preserve man's free moral agency, which they conclude is in jeopardy if God truly has foreknowledge of the future, contingent, free will choices of men. In other words, accepting Calvin's premise, they then argue the flip-side of the same theological coin. I, on the other hand, totally reject Calvinism, including his beginning premise, which is more than I can say for some of my brethren. Even so, I have never considered these brethren to be proto-, neo-, or crypto-Calvinists. Accordingly, it would be helpful if some would find out just what

Calvinism is before haphazardly bandying about their uninformed recriminations. Brethren, it is nothing short of sinful to fling about accusations without a shred of evidence. If someone is teaching false doctrine, there must be proof. If we don't have the proof, then we had better not make the charge. A charge without proof is, in essence, bearing false witness.[19] It should be obvious that I am not against speaking out against false teaching or teachers. What I am against is the ungodly way it is *sometimes* done. In fact, I am absolutely dismayed at the shoddy and underhanded way some brethren conduct themselves in controversy. No one, not even a false teacher, must ever be charged with anything that cannot be proven. The fact that this sort of behavior is becoming all too commonplace in religious discussions and disagreements is a shame and disgrace!

Calvin was wrong, and so are my brethren who believe God's foreknowledge and man's free will are incompatible. Frankly, fairness and integrity demand that those who believe this alleged incompatibility to be self-evident are under obligation to prove it, not just assume it or assert it. In truth, this supposed incompatibility has never been proven, and it never will be. Even so, some persist in arguing that if God actually knows the future before it happens, then it is *certain* to happen; thus, the freedom and contingency of the future are totally shattered. They then advance the idea that the certainty of future events and actions make them *fixed*, and if they are "fixed," then man can do nothing other than what has been certain or fixed from eternity. Now, if one accepts this line of reasoning, and I certainly don't, then he has but two choices: (1) he becomes a Calvinist or some other kind of

---

[19] See Romans 13:9.

determinist or (2) he denies God's foreknowledge of the future, contingent, free will acts of His creatures.

Many contemporary theologians have opted for the latter. Among these are Richard Rice, who we mentioned earlier, and Richard Swinburne, who wrote:

> *If God is omniscient then he foreknows all future human actions. If God foreknows anything, then it will necessarily come to pass. But if a human action will necessarily come to pass, then it cannot be free.*[20]

Believing, though, that man is free, Swinburne proposes a "modified account of omniscience."[21] This is the same thing Rice has done. Together, they argue in favor of God's all-knowingness, but excluding from this all-knowingness any and all "future, contingent, free will choices." God's omniscience, they insist, includes all there is to know, but this does not include future free will acts because these acts are simply not knowable. I mentioned this earlier, but have repeated it here for obvious reasons. Unfortunately, Rice and Swinburne, along with some of my brethren, have become so enamored with man-made philosophies that they have, as a result, created a sham god who is much different than the one true God of the Bible. Questioned about their obvious idolatry, they have tried to protect their theological creation by masquerading him behind the cover of orthotalksy.

If we accept their major premise, then man-made philosophies do, indeed, sound very logical and, therefore, correct. Yes, God does foreknow the future and, therefore, the future He foreknows is going to happen. Yes, one can argue that the future is, indeed,

---

[20] Richard Swinburne, *The Coherence of Theism*, 1977, page 167.
[21] Swineburne, pages 172ff.

"fixed." But the path these folks have chosen at this point leads away from scriptural truths. Yes, the future acts of men and women are "fixed" all right, but not in any *causative* sense. In other words, they are "fixed" not because of God's foreknowledge, but because this is the way free moral agents, exercising their free will choices, will choose to act in the future, and God, simply because He is who He is, foreknows them. This view, contrary to those of Rice, Swinburne *et al.*, is totally consistent with what the Bible says about the complete compatibility of God's foreknowledge and man's free will. Regrettably, some are more swayed by the think-sos of men than the truths taught in God's Word.

Chapter 7

The God Who Can Fail

Have you not known? Have you not heard? The everlasting God, the Lord, the Creator of the ends of the earth, neither faints nor is weary. His understanding is unsearchable. He gives power to the weak, and to those who have no might He increases strength. Even the youths shall faint and be weary, and the young men shall utterly fall, but those who wait on the Lord shall renew their strength; they shall mount up with wings like eagles, they shall run and not be weary, they shall walk and not faint (Isaiah 40:28-31).

For those who believe in a God who is omnipotent, it may sound very strange to hear someone teaching that God can fail. Of course, this is exactly the idea being formulated by Process theologians and some New Testament Christians. I first heard this idea being actively expressed by brethren almost twenty years ago. Who and where are not important to this study. In all fairness, let me say that I do not believe any of these people, and this includes the process folks, advocate their position out of animosity toward the one true God. The problem, once again, is the free will issue. It is unfortunate that something so wonderful (viz., free moral agency) can be so misused by the evil one. Even so, we have learned by now that the Devil is a master at perverting things that, in and of themselves, are wonderful and good. Actually, God's gracious gift of free will, which is the key to understanding so much that transpires between God and His creatures, is sorely misunderstood by many people. Consequently, before proceeding further, permit me to make a needed observation or two.

If man is truly free, if only in a limited sense, then God's power is limited. For instance, God cannot (unless you hold the determinist view) force someone to obey the gospel. Why? Because man has free will, and if man has free will, then God, no matter how powerful He is, cannot make (in a determinist sense) a free moral agent obey Him. If this is true (and again, only a determinist would deny it), then there are some things an all-powerful God cannot do. But, please, don't panic. This truth is not quite the breeding ground for error that you might think. Any self-imposed limitation that God might place upon Himself is not actually a limitation at all, ontologically speaking. For example, the Bible makes it clear that God cannot lie.[1] Does this impinge on His omnipotence? No, God is still omnipotent—that is, He can accomplish (make happen) anything He purposes to accomplish (make happen)—even though He cannot lie. Further, the things God cannot do are not limitations imposed upon Him from outside of Himself. If they were, of course, then they would negate His omnipotence. God is limited only by the necessity of being *He Who Is Who He Is* and the free exercise of His own will; neither of which abrogate His all-powerfulness. That He has freely chosen to be limited by the free moral agency of His creatures—the very creation of which necessitated omnipotence—does not nullify His omnipotence. In fact, it serves only to enhance and glorify it. Indeed, we join with the heavenly host in saying: "Alleluia! For the Lord God Omnipotent reigns!"[2]

Rice, Swinburne *et al.*, argue that because His creatures have free will, God does not have foreknowledge of their future,

---

[1] See Titus 1:2.
[2] Revelation 19:6.

contingent, free will choices.[3] If this is true, they argue, then God is limited in what He can do. He can, for instance, determine to redeem fallen man, He can even implement the plan, but He cannot actually know whether the plan will be successful because of the free moral agency of those who are the objects of the plan. I know of several well-known gospel preachers who teach this. Specifically, they teach that God's plan to redeem man through His Son, Jesus Christ, could have failed. Quite frankly, the first time I heard one of these "God can't know what can't be known, therefore, God could have failed" brothers teach this doctrine, I was shocked. I have now heard it articulated enough that I am not quite as shocked as I was at the beginning. Even so, I am still troubled every time I hear this erroneous argument expressed.

In essence, this doctrine teaches that Jesus Christ was not *the* plan, as the Bible teaches, but was, instead, *a* plan. If the Son would have failed in His mission to redeem fallen man, then according to these brethren, the Father would have had to implement some other strategy to salvage His original Scheme of Redemption. But what other strategy? If Jesus would have failed in His mission, then God in the flesh would have failed. As the whole undertaking was, in fact, the Father's plan, then He, too, would have failed. For the sake of argument and clarification, let's indulge this theological delusion for a moment so that we can discover its inescapable conclusion.

Speculating, one might say that even though the Father and Son were unable to effect man's salvation, maybe the Holy Spirit would be able to come up with a plan to redeem man. But, by this

---

[3] It has already been demonstrated that this idea is not only contrary to the Scriptures, but is nothing more than an unproved philosophical assumption.

time, the Godhead (viz., the Father, Son, and Holy Spirit) would have been corrupted by sin and failure. *Ergo*, the triune God, the one who revealed Himself to us in the Bible, would no longer exist—He would have decayed, or disintegrated, or whatever happens to a sham god of this sort. Brethren, this sort of theological gibberish cannot be right. But unfortunately, not only do some preachers believe and preach this, they are even considered by some to be the epitome of true wisdom and orthodoxy.

The Scheme of Redemption was "predestined according to the purpose of Him who works all things according to the counsel of His will."[4] Does this sound like a plan that could fail? Certainly not! Nevertheless, the plan would be no mean undertaking. It would ultimately take the sacrifice of the heavenly Father's only begotten Son,[5] the divine *Logos*,[6] who would sooner or later have to leave heaven, take upon Himself the mantle of flesh,[7] and finally shed His blood on the cruel cross of Calvary for the remission of our sins.[8] As such, this was not simply *a* plan—it was, instead, *the* plan. It was the plan that would work because God's foreknowledge would allow Him to not just design a plan that *could*, under certain circumstances, work, but it would also allow Him to carry out the plan with absolutely impeccable precision.[9] As the result of this perfect plan, the heavenly Father would be able to "bring many sons unto glory."[10] This plan could not, and would not, fail.

---

[4] Ephesians 1:11.
[5] See John 3:16-18.
[6] See John 3:16-18.
[7] See John 1:14.
[8] See Matthew 26:28.
[9] See Acts 2:23.
[10] Hebrews 2:9-10.

How can I be so sure? Because, it was God's plan, and He is the one who said:

> *Remember the former things of old, for I am God, and there is no other; I am God, and there is none like Me, declaring the end from the beginning, and from ancient times things that are not yet done, saying, 'My counsel shall stand, and I will do all My pleasure,' calling a bird of prey from the east, the man who executes My counsel, from a far country. Indeed I have spoken it; I will also bring it to pass. I have purposed it; I will also do it.*[11]

Does this sound like a God who could fail? Again, in Proverbs 19:21, the Scriptures say: "There are many plans in a man's heart, nevertheless the Lord's counsel—that will stand."

The Scheme of Redemption originated in, and will eventually culminate in, eternity:

> *For whom He foreknew, He also predestined to be conformed to the image of His Son, that He might be the firstborn among many brethren. Moreover whom He predestined, these He also called; whom He called, these He also justified; and whom He justified, these He also glorified.*[12]

Hence, in the mind of God, and this is a mind that knows the future, contingent, free will choices of men and women, the Scheme of Redemption is a "done deal." Now, please do not misunderstand me. I am not talking about a done deal the way the Calvinists contend. Although the Greek word *proorizo*, translated in the KJV as "predestinate," does mean, according to *Strong's Greek and Hebrew Lexicon*, to "predetermine," "decide beforehand," or "foreordain,"

---

[11] Isaiah 46:9-11.
[12] Romans 8:29-30.

this does not mean that God, in eternity, made a choice of those He would save independent of anything they would do of their own free wills. Rather, God ordained or decreed, in eternity (i.e., He predestined), that those who were going be saved would have to be conformed to the image of His Son.[13] This means that God did not choose individuals to be saved *unconditionally*, as Calvinism teaches. Instead, based upon His foreknowledge of the future, contingent, free will choices of His creatures, God predestined (i.e., determined beforehand) those who would be saved *conditionally* (viz., the condition being conformity to His Son's image). This is what the apostle Paul was writing about when he said: "...just as He [the Father] chose us in Him [Jesus Christ] before the foundation of the world, that we should be holy and without blame before Him in love, having predestined us to adoption as sons by Jesus Christ to Himself, according to the good pleasure of His will."[14] Again, does this sound like a plan that could have failed?

Acts 2:23 is the key to understanding the dichotomy that some think exists between foreknowledge and free will. It demonstrates how God works through His foreknowledge and is the perfect illustration of why God cannot fail. The passage says: "Him, being delivered by the determinate counsel and foreknowledge of God, you have taken by lawless hands, have crucified, and put to death." This passage does not teach that God's foreknowledge depends upon His determinate counsel, as determinists, and some of my brethren, teach. What this passage really says is that the death of Jesus happened the way it did because of God's predetermined plan and foreknowledge. Both of these factors were involved in Jesus' death on the cross. On the one hand, God determined that Jesus

---

[13] See Romans 8:29.
[14] Ephesians 1:4-5.

would become the propitiation for the sins of the world. On the other hand, the details of how this would be accomplished were planned in connection with God's foreknowledge of the historical situation and the character and free will choices of men like Judas and the other actors in this real-life drama. In Acts 4:27-28, the Bible says, "For truly against Your holy Servant Jesus, whom You anointed, both Herod and Pontius Pilate, with the Gentiles and the people of Israel, were gathered together to do whatever Your hand and Your purpose determined before to be done." Therefore, if man is truly a free moral agent, and the Bible says he is, then God's foreknowledge of the future, contingent, free will choices of men and women is the only way He could have carried out His predetermined plan without destroying man's free will.

The Bible says that the same foreknowledge that allowed God to know His plan for redeeming fallen man would not fail[15] is the same foreknowledge that allowed Him to know that "many sons" would, in fact, be brought to glory.[16] I believe the "glory" in this verse is equivalent to the "glory" of 2 Corinthians 3:18 and is, therefore, the eternal glory that we, if we remain faithful, will one day share with our glorified Lord in heaven.[17] Now, if God does not have actual foreknowledge of the future, contingent, free will choices of men, as some are claiming, then how could He possibly have known that there would be *any* sons who would be brought to glory? But God actually speaks of "many sons" in Hebrews 2:10 and "many brethren" in Romans 8:29, the mentioning of which speaks conclusively regarding His actual foreknowledge of the future, contingent, free will choices of men and women. The

---

[15] See Acts 2:23.
[16] See Hebrews 2:10.
[17] See Romans 8:18-23; 2 Corinthians 4:17-5:5; Philippians 3:20-21; Colossians 3:4; 1 Peter 5:1-4,10.

immediate context of these two passages makes this a *necessary conclusion*, which is as binding as any *direct statement* or *approved example* derived from God's Word.

If God does not have actual foreknowledge of the future, contingent, free will choices of men, that is, if He is truly a God who can fail, then He is nothing more than a sham God whose claim of superiority over the false gods of paganism is nothing but deception and fraud,[18] all of which makes Him but little more than the two-faced, impotent, and very finite Wizard of Oz. "No," a thousand times "No." For such a God could not be YHWH, the Almighty God, the I Am that I Am, the Creator, Sustainer, and Savior of the universe! As the true God said in Isaiah 40:28-31:

> *Have you not known? Have you not heard? The everlasting God, the Lord, the Creator of the ends of the earth, neither faints nor is weary. His understanding is unsearchable. He gives power to the weak, and to those who have no might He increases strength. Even the youths shall faint and be weary, and the young men shall utterly fall, but those who wait on the Lord shall renew their strength; they shall mount up with wings like eagles, they shall run and not be weary, they shall walk and not faint.*

The God of the Bible does not—indeed, He cannot—fail! Anyone who thinks He can is wrong. Furthermore, anyone who thinks He can, while giving lip-service to His omnipotence and omniscience is engaged in orthotalksy. Remember, idols are not just found on pagan altars, but in the hearts and minds of well-educated men and women as well.

---

[18] See Isaiah 41:21-29.

Chapter 8

The God Who Can Cease Being God

If I have told you earthly things and you do not believe, how will you believe if I tell you heavenly things? No one has ascended to heaven but He who came down from heaven, that is, the Son of Man who is in heaven (John 3:12-13).

The ruckus taking place in the church today over the Deity of Jesus is all the evidence needed to prove that some Christians actually believe that God can cease being God. That there are brethren who believe that the *Divine Logos*, in order to become a man,[1] divested Himself of His Divinity and Godhood cannot be doubted. Although one who had publicly espoused this idea has now acknowledged his error, nevertheless, there are numerous others who still believe it. It is my firm conviction that this issue is the most serious threat to the integrity of Christianity that has occurred in the modern era. Consequently, it has troubled me greatly that many Christians consider the whole controversy over the Deity of Jesus to be a preacher squabble about a subject that is just not all that important. Brethren, Jesus clearly said, "If you do not believe that I am He, you will die in your sins."[2] When He said this, He was not arguing for His humanity. On the contrary, He

---

[1] See John 1:1,14.
[2] John 8:24.

was saying that if one did not believe in His Deity, he could not go to heaven. The apostle John identifies this as the spirit of "Anti-christ."[3] Therefore, the question over the Deity of Jesus is not a "tempest in a teapot" issue. Where you and I will spend eternity depends upon getting this answer right!

For Christianity to be what it is, there are two cardinal tenets that cannot be tampered with: (1) the Incarnation of God's Son, and (2) the triune nature of the Godhead. If Jesus Christ is, in fact, the eternal, divine Word of God the Father, and if the unity of God is taken seriously,[4] then a plurality of persons within the Godhead is a fact that cannot be denied. In fact, if it had not been for the Incarnation, the truth about the triune nature of God would have never arisen. Hence, the truth about the Deity of Jesus and the Godhead are necessarily interconnected doctrines of the Christian faith. If one were to refute either of these doctrines, then Christianity would be shown to be nothing more than an elaborately devised sham. So, when one, for whatever reason, begins to argue that God the Son divested His Godhood and Divinity and became just a man, he has become, whether he thinks so or not, an enemy of the faith. Undoubtedly, an intrinsically human Jesus is nothing more than a sham god. When those who have created this gelded god then turn around and proclaim to believe in his Deity, they are engaged in orthotalksy.

Those among us who argue for a totally human Jesus (with Deity divested) are reflecting the influence of process theology, which proudly asserts that the classical two-natures doctrine of Jesus presupposes concepts that are outdated, absurd, and totally irrelevant to the modern way of thinking. According to the Processians,

---

[3] 1 John 4:3.
[4] See John 1:1.

Jesus as the God-man is a concept that must go, because it is not possible for the sophisticated, enlightened mind to believe the impossibly absurd idea that two entities (God and man) can occupy the same space at the same time. In other words, when viewed as substances, Deity cannot possibly unite with humanity without creating the displacement of one substance by the other. One can be God, or one can be man, but one cannot be both God and man simultaneously. Processians love to talk about the "havoc" wreaked by the belief that Jesus of Nazareth was both fully God and fully man at the same time. This is, of course, precisely the same idea being expressed by some brethren today, who scoff at the idea that Jesus could be 100% God and 100% man without being a 200% monstrosity. Therefore, when I listen to or read after these brethren, I want to ask, "Will the real Processians among us please stand up?"

Given the nature of God, there is no chance that He can ever be anything other that what He is. This can be inferred from His self-existent, eternal, and infinite nature. His nature or essence cannot change, but is eternally the same, incorruptible[5] and immortal.[6] In other words, He is unchangeable or immutable.[7] What does this mean? It means that the Self-Existent One cannot be not self-existent; it means that the Eternal One cannot be not eternal; it means that the Infinite One cannot be not infinite; *et cetera*. God, ontologically speaking (i.e., by the nature of His being), cannot be anything else; if He were, He would not be God.

Included in God's unchangeable or immutable nature are His moral attributes, for His moral character is no less a part of His

---

[5] See Romans 1:23.
[6] See 1 Timothy 6:16.
[7] Psalm 102:25-27; Malachi 3:6; James 1:17.

essence than are His power and wisdom. What this means is that God has always been, and always will be, the holy, righteous and gracious God that He is right at this moment. His goodness has not been developed and it will never be altered. From everlasting to everlasting, He is the same in character, infallible and immutable.[8]

Of course, it must be kept in mind that the immutability of God's nature does not mean that He cannot interact with His creation. As was pointed out previously, the Bible teaches that the Almighty has agreed to, and does, interact with His creation in the **now** of time. Such interaction is genuine and not pretended. God has agreed to be influenced by His creation. Whether or not I can explain this in view of God's immutable nature is not the point. I cannot even understand it; how, then, can I explain it? In truth, it is not my responsibility to explain it; it is, instead, my responsibility to believe, teach, and defend it. If I had to be able to understand and explain everything about God, especially those things He has not chosen to reveal to me, before I could believe in Him, I and every other finite creature could have no choice but to remain in unbelief.

It is not possible that the essence of God could be anything other than what it has been, is, and always will be. If this essence were to change, then God would no longer be God. As a matter of fact, it is impossible to make distinctions between God, His essence and His attributes. "I Am that I Am" or "He who is"[9] exists

---

[8] See Numbers 23:19.
[9] Exodus 3:14.

as a self-existent,[10] eternal,[11] infinite,[12] immutable[13] Spirit.[14] *If He ceased to be any of these, He could not be God.* God's essence (i.e., that which makes Him what He is) could not be anything other than what it is; and that which makes God what He is, of course, is His attributes. Therefore, it is never correct to think of God apart from His essence or attributes. This means that God does not have an essence; He is His essence, and He does not have attributes; He is His attributes.

For example, and I mentioned this back in chapter two, the Bible tells us that God is love.[15] It informs us that God's love is great,[16] eternal,[17] infinite,[18] and dependable.[19] If the theme of the Bible is man's redemption, then the central word of the Bible is love. In fact, the Bible tells us that the motivation for the scheme of redemption is God's love for His creation. How much did God love His creation? He loved it so much that He was willing to give His only begotten Son so that it could be redeemed.[20] But what kind of love would do such a thing? To understand this, we must realize that God's love for mankind is a distinctive kind of love called *agape*. And what is *agape*? Primarily, *agape* is good will toward others. It is deep, tender, and warm concern for the happiness and well-being of another; it is charity toward those in need.

---

[10] See Romans 1:23; 1 Timothy 6:16; John 5:26.
[11] See Deuteronomy 33:27.
[12] See Psalm 139:7-10; Isaiah 46:9,10; Jeremiah 32:27.
[13] See Psalm 102:25-27; Malachi 3:6; James 1:17.
[14] See John 4:24.
[15] See 1 John 4:8,16.
[16] See Ephesians 2:4.
[17] See Jeremiah 31:3; Ephesians 1:4,5.
[18] See Ephesians 3:18,19.
[19] See Romans 8:35-39.
[20] See John 3:16; 1 John 4:9.

Again, when the Bible says, "God loves us," it means that He really cares about us and always does what is best for us. God's love is different from other kinds of love in that it seeks to give and not to get; it seeks to satisfy not some need of the lover, but rather the need of the one who is loved. This is what God is, that is, this is His nature. Strip from God His love and we no longer have the God who has revealed Himself to His creatures. Strip from Him His love and what remains is something very similar to the gods of the pagans.

Finally, what the Bible does not say about the essence or nature of God is just as important as what it does say. For instance, although the Bible teaches that God is His attributes and characteristics, it does not teach that any particular attribute of God is God. In other words, the Bible is not saying, and has never said, that "Love is God." On the contrary, the Bible teaches that "God is love" (I John 4:8,16). Clearly, then, the Bible instructs us that God is His attributes and characteristics. Anyone who believes the Bible believes this. Consequently, God is, has been, and always will be who and what He is at this exact moment.

Jesus is God. This is the basic meaning of the Incarnation. In John 1:1, the Holy Spirit teaches that not only was the Word (i.e., the *Divine Logos*) in the beginning with God, but the Word was God. In verses 14-34, we learn that the Logos became flesh in the person of Jesus of Nazareth. In a book written so that men would believe that Jesus is the Christ, the Son of God, and believing might have life in His name, Thomas, speaking of Jesus, exclaims, after seeing Him in His resurrected body, "My Lord and my God."[21] There are, of course, other passages that directly speak of Jesus as God, but since they are all disputed by some, I have chosen

---

[21] John 20:28.

not to mention them here. Nevertheless, the cited passages serve to demonstrate, to those who are willing to believe the Bible, that Jesus is, in fact, God.

Furthermore, the writer of Hebrews, telling us what God had prophesied about Jesus, writes, "But to the Son He says: 'Your throne, O God, is forever and ever.'"[22] He also clearly identifies Jesus as the Jehovah and Elohim of Psalm 102:25-27, who eternally existed before He created the heavens and earth[23] and who remains eternally the same[24] and, therefore, in the person of Jesus Christ is "the same yesterday, today, and forever."[25] To see in Hebrews 13:8 only a reference to the faithfulness of Jesus, and not a reference to His immutability, is a serious mistake. In fact, Jesus Christ's faithfulness is grounded in His changelessness. Because He does not change ontologically (i.e., because He has always been the fullness of God that He is at this very moment), He has been, is, and always will be, completely and totally reliable. It is only in this sense that Jesus could identify Himself as the "I Am that I Am" or "He who is" of Exodus 3:14.[26] When Jesus said, "Most assuredly, I say to you, before Abraham was, I Am," He used the aorist tense to describe Abraham's existence and the timeless present tense to describe His own existence, and thereby identified Himself as the self-existent, eternal, infinite, immutable God with a capital "G."

Lord, You have been our dwelling place in all generations. Before the mountains were brought forth, or ever You had formed

---

[22] Hebrews 1:8.
[23] See Hebrews 1:10.
[24] See Hebrews 1:11,12.
[25] Hebrews 13:8.
[26] See John 8:58.

the earth and the world, even from everlasting to everlasting, You are God.[27]

As difficult as it may be for finite creatures to even begin to comprehend (the Bible calls it a mystery in 1 Timothy 3:16), when the *Divine Logos* or Son of God became flesh,[28] or came in the likeness of man,[29] or was manifested in the flesh,[30] He did not divest, give up, or have stripped from Him, His Deity. Within the man Jesus of Nazareth dwelt, and continues to dwell (for such is the meaning of the present tense), all (not some of) the fullness of the Godhead bodily.[31] From a Biblical standpoint, the historical Jesus is never understood apart from His embodiment as the self-existent, eternal, infinite, immutable God in time and space. One might argue that a God divested of His Deity would still continue to exist; but, if He did, He would no longer be what He had been and, therefore, would not be entitled to call Himself "I Am that I Am."

When Jesus identified Himself with the enduring 'I' of Exodus 3:14,[32] He was not just claiming to have been God previously. Instead, He was claiming to be the eternal 'I.' To those who rejected His Deity, He said:

Even if I bear witness of Myself, My witness is true, for I know where I came from and where I am going; but you do not know

---

[27] Psalm 90:1,2.
[28] See John 1:14.
[29] See Philippians 2:8.
[30] See 1 Timothy 3:16.
[31] See Colossians 2:9.
[32] See John 8:58.

*where I come from and where I am going. You judge according to the flesh...[some translations say, 'by human standards'].*³³

Brethren are creating a sham god and engaging in orthotalksy because they are trying to rely on their human understanding. Reason *alone*, unaided by divine revelation, provides a knowledge of God that is, at its best, only partial and, at its worst, frequently in error.³⁴ Philosophy simply does not lend itself to an adequate understanding of God's hidden character and purposes.³⁵ God—*who* He is and *what* He is—is not understood on the basis of human speculation, but by the explicit teachings of the God-breathed Word. In other words, "If anyone speaks, let him speak as the oracles of God."³⁶

---

³³ John 8:14-15.
³⁴ See 1 Corinthians 2:6-14.
³⁵ See 1 Corinthians 1:21-25.
³⁶ 1 Peter 4:11.

Chapter 9

The God Who Must Be Either Here Or There

Where can I go from Your Spirit? Or where can I flee from your presence? If I ascend into heaven, You are there. If I take the wings of the morning, and dwell in the uttermost parts of the sea, even there Your hand shall lead me, and Your right hand shall hold me (Psalm 139:7-10).

Looking at the title of this chapter, you might be thinking, "Who among us could believe such a thing?" Well, if my experiences are indicative of brotherhood norms, then there are more than a few New Testament Christians who think this way. But before proceeding further, I want to make it clear that I do not think my fellow Christians who think this way are intentionally trying to create a sham god. Absolutely not! Nevertheless, this is what they do when they argue that the actual indwelling of the Holy Spirit in every obedient believer could only be accomplished by either a fragmented or multi-located Holy Spirit. By this they mean that if the indwelling of the Holy Spirit in every Christian is *actual*, rather than "only in and through the Word," as they are wont to say, then this could only be accomplished by either breaking (or dividing into pieces) the Holy Spirit, or by means of a multi-located Holy Spirit (i.e., a Holy Spirit that could be in more than one place at the same time, an idea they think is absurd).

One who takes this position accused me of believing that "the Holy Spirit is scattered, one-to-a-believer, into thousands, perhaps millions, of fully functional, self-contained, independent units, each one the perfect clone of all the others." Of course, this caricature does not represent what I believe, as such would be polytheism, pure and simple. But it does represent the kind of maneuvering that goes on in the minds of those who think God is somehow limited by space.

As I've pointed out time and again in this study, the one true God is infinite in His characteristics and attributes. This means He is not restricted by any *external* limitations, which does not include, of course, those internal limitations He may place on Himself or which are due to His nature. Therefore, this infinitude is defined by God's self-existence, eternalness and omni-characterictics, which are omnipresence, omniscience and omnipotence. If we, in our theological surmisings, try to take any of these away from Him, then we honor a god who could no longer be the God of the Bible. Instead, he (and I've purposely dropped the capitalization here) becomes just another of the sham gods of orthotalksy.

Why then do otherwise faithful, intelligent Christians engage in such shenanigans? I don't know all the reasons, but in some cases, at least, they think themselves to be defending *the* faith once and for all delivered[1] against whatever false "ism" they happen to be zeroing in on at the moment. This means they never see themselves as anything else but faithful to the Lord and His Word. In reference to the Holy Spirit, this "ism" is most often Pentecostalism. As one who has taught and helped to convert many Pentecostals, I certainly understand the many errors associated with it. But when one thinks he is defending the faith by denigrating the characteristics and attributes of God, then it seems to me that these folks have involved themselves in an equally terrible delusion. Yes,

---

[1] See Jude 3.

Pentecostals are wrong about the Holy Spirit, seemingly unable to decide whether He's a "He" or an "it." They fail to distinguish between the *indwelling* of the Holy Spirit, the *baptism* of the Holy Spirit and the *gifts* of the Holy Spirit. They readily misappropriate passages to teach that all Christians are to be directly guided by the Holy Spirit. They believe the miraculous manifestations ("gifts") of the Spirit are continuing today, even after that which is perfect has come—that is, the completed Word of God.[2] There are, in fact, a whole host of errors associated with Pentecostalism. But to diminish God's infinitude in the name of fighting Pentecostalism is a gross error that causes one, however unintentionally, to imbibe idolatry.

Theologians have argued that "God, in the totality of his essence, without diffusion or expansion, multiplication or division, penetrates and fills the universe in all its parts."[3] Although I do not feel the need to defend anyone's theological construct but my own (and I am aware that my thinking could itself be in error), I do think this quote accurately represents the nature of omnipresence as set forth in the Bible.[4] However, I wish to make it understood that I totally reject the idea of Pantheism, a concept that says everything is God and God is everything (i.e., that the material universe somehow makes up the very fabric of God). I make this disclaimer because several over the years have accused me of being a pantheist. More than likely, these charges were made by those who have never even talked to or, what's more, helped convert a pantheist. Unfortunately, pantheism is a terribly wrong concept that presently enslaves more than a billion people, and I feel blessed to have

---

[2] See 1 Corinthians 13:8-13.
[3] See Cottrell, *What The Bible Says About God The Creator*, pages 264-273.
[4] See Psalm 139:7-10; Jeremiah 23:23-24; 1 Kings 8:27.

taught and helped to convert more than a few pantheists. No, the uncreated, self-existent, eternal Creator is not some pantheistic everything. He does not consist of that which He has created. Instead, He stands above and beyond that which He's created. Consequently, the transcendent God is not limited by the space-time continuum and is not, therefore, a spatial being (viz., He transcends all spatial limitations).

All Created Beings Are Spatial Creatures

Space, like time, is a product of creation. Therefore, all created beings are spatial creatures. This means that both the material and spiritual dimensions are spatial, though not necessarily in the same way. Although spiritual "space" is obviously not like material space, each of these dimensions must, by nature of their creation, have spatial limitations. Consequently, space of some sort is characteristic of all created beings.

The material universe of which we humans are a part is three-dimensional space. Our bodies themselves are spatial and, therefore, limited by the three-dimensional boundaries of space. Included in these limitation are the following: a material body can exist in only one space at a time; to get from one space to another, a material body must pass through the intervening space. This means that given the limitations of three dimensional space, it is *impossible*, when we factor in the fourth dimension of time, for a material body to occupy two different spaces at the same time.

In contrast to this, and evidently at the same time, *fully* spiritual creatures, such as angels and demons, do not normally occupy our space, as we do.[5] Therefore, it can be safely concluded that these

---

[5] See Jude 6.

spiritual creatures are not restricted by the limitations of three-dimensional space, as we are. Nevertheless, as created beings, they have their own spatial dimension, with whatever limits that exist there. As I don't occupy that dimension, I can't tell you what it is like, but that this dimension exists is evident from Scripture. Further, the Bible teaches that when these spiritual creatures interact with material space, they are not totally outside its limits. For example, a spiritual creature, although he can evidently act multi-dimensional, can still only be in one space at a time. This is illustrated by the angelic appearance recorded in Daniel 10. The prophet Daniel had been "mourning" (which clearly included praying) for "three full weeks" (verse 2). When the angel appeared, he said:

> *Do not fear, Daniel, for from the first day that you set your heart to understand, and to humble yourself before your God, your words were heard; and I have come because of your words. But the prince of the kingdom of Persia withstood me twenty-one days; and behold, Michael, one of the chief princes, came to help me, for I had been left alone there with the kings of Persia.*[6]

He went on to say, "Now I have come to make you understand what will happen to your people in the latter days, for the vision refers to many days yet to come" (verse 14).

So, when interacting with our material dimension, this angel could not be in two places at the same time. He had been sent to answer Daniel and make known to him what would happen to his people in the future, but the "prince of Persia" (evidently another spiritual entity) withstood him for "twenty-one days." The struggle was so intense that Michael (another spiritual creature) had to

---

[6] Daniel 10:12-13.

come and help him. Then, after administering to Daniel, he still needed to return and "fight" with the prince of Persia, knowing that the "prince of Greece" would eventually be involved (verse 20).

It is clear from Scripture, then, that a spiritual creature cannot occupy more than one space at a time. This means that spiritual beings (angels and demons) are not omnipresent. Satan himself cannot be everywhere at once and therefore uses other spiritual entities to represent his interests around the world.

What all this means, as I've said before, is that created beings, whether they be spiritual or material, are spatial beings. But in complete contrast to His creation, God, the uncreated Creator, is not a spatial being. He is unlimited by space and is, in fact, transcendent by means of His infinitude. The traditional word for this is *immensity*. However, because this word has come to mean "very large in size," one must be very careful to exclude this connotation when speaking of God.

God is not immensely large, so as to fill all of space, even to infinity. Such thinking would be totally false and is manifested in Pantheism. The word itself literally means unmeasurable, not because God is too large to measure, but because, as a non-spatial being, He is not the kind of Being that can be measured. The term simply means that God is not limited by space. As such, all the limitations of space—extension, location and distance—simply do not apply to Him.

Therefore, God is universally present to all of space at all times. This does not mean, however, that He is dispersed throughout the infinite reaches of space, so that every part of space has at least a little part of God. God is not present *in* all of space, which is pantheism; instead, He is present *to* all of space. This means that the unlimited God in His whole Being is present at every point of our space. Perhaps a better way of saying this is to say that all space is immediately present before God. Personally, I don't care how you look at this as long as you understand that the God who has revealed Himself in the Bible is not limited by space, as are His creatures.

Now, before going further, it is important to point out that I do not believe everyone who disagrees with me on the *actual* indwelling of the Holy Spirit in the body of every obedient believer is engaged in idolatry. Certainly not! I have fellowship with those who think the Holy Spirit dwells in the Christian *only in and through the word*. In fact, I believe it fair to say that the majority of brethren I have associated with over the years believe this way. They could be right, although I do not think so. Nevertheless, neither the integrity of God nor His Word (viz., the Holy Scriptures) suffers from such a conclusion, and as long as my fellow Christians do not withdraw from me due to my position, then I expect continued fellowship with those who disagree with me on this compelling subject. But my humble opinion, for those who haven't quite figured it out yet, is that the Holy Spirit actually dwells in the physical bodies of Christians.[7]

However, when some, in order to defend their position that the Holy Spirit indwells the Christian only in and through the Word, begin to make God in man's image, subject to the same limitations as the creatures He created, I wish to make it clear that such are engaged in idolatry. In my opinion, there is no excuse for such thinking. Nevertheless, teachers of God's Word, seemingly without any embarrassment at all, make all sorts of spatial-limiting arguments for why it is supposedly impossible for the Holy Spirit to actually and equally occupy all the bodies of all obedient believers.

---

[7] See 1 Corinthians 3:19 and 3:16-17.

I believe at least some of the reasons for this is that, unfortunately, many Christians today have drunk deeply at the humanist-materialist well. These give lip-service to omnipresence, but then define it in such a way as to effectively deny it. This is, as I've said, nothing but orthotalksy. If God is omnipresent, then don't expect me to be impressed by arguments that claim He can't be in more than one place at a time, and if He were, He'd be divided into pieces (or clones) of Himself. This is not just poppycock, but is a manifestation of unbelief, and anyone who claims to be a teacher of God's Word while making such a claim ought to be ashamed of himself.

It needs to be understood that God's omnipresence does not prevent Him from manifesting Himself in a localized place. In fact, while it is true that His ontological Being is present *to* all of space equally, He has, at various times and for various reasons, entered space at specific points and become present *in* it. These "theophanies," as they are called, most often involved redemption. There was, for instance, the account of God's presence in the garden of Eden "in the cool of the evening."[8] There was His appearance before the Israelites as a pillar of cloud by day and fire by night.[9] Of course, the most dramatic case of God entering time and space was the Incarnation itself.[10] But, and this point needs to be clearly understood, in entering time and space, God, in His self-existent, eternal and infinite Being, did not cease to be omnipresent. He was, while existing as Jesus of Nazareth, still present to every point of space and was, in fact, holding everything together by the "word of

---

[8] Genesis 3:8ff.
[9] See Exodus 33:9; 40:34; 1 Kings 8:10ff.
[10] See John 1:14; 1 Timothy 3:16.

His power."[11] With this in mind, it seems evident that the omnipresence of Immanuel or "God with us" is the real subject of John 3:13, which says, "No one has ascended to heaven but He who came down from heaven, that is, the Son of God who is in heaven."

I've heard people say they didn't know what this passage was saying, but they knew it couldn't mean what folks like me think it means. This isn't exactly cogent exegesis, if you ask me. Nevertheless, some among us are confident that the ontological presence of the Word, who was Himself God, could not be on earth, in the body of Jesus of Nazareth, and be in heaven at the same time. I suppose it could be that this difficult passage is not saying what I think it's saying, but the teacher of God's Word who claims that it "can't be" is clearly not taking into consideration the omnipresence of Jehovah's ontological Being—a Being not limited by time and space. Yes, I know the concept is mind-boggling, but such is, I believe, characteristic of the magnificent nature of Almighty God. When contemplating the nature of God, it is not detrimental to have our minds boggled a bit.

It has been my experience that when one moves off of center on a particular Bible subject, he's probably off on something else as well. Why? Because the Word of God, which is "profitable for doctrine, for reproof, for correction, for instruction in righteousness"[12] is a palliative against false doctrine. If we take a wrong position on something, we can be sure other passages will confront our wrong interpretation and, if we are amenable, they will surely correct our error. However, when we come to a conclusion that a particular interpretation is right, and we are unwilling to be corrected,

---

[11] Hebrews 1:3; cf. Colossians 1:17.
[12] 2 Timothy 3:16f.

convinced beyond all doubt that our position is the right one, we will surely have to misinterpret and misapply other passages that impinge our belief. In other words, the Word of God, if we will let it, when properly understood and believed, will make us "complete, thoroughly equipped for every good work."[13] The starting point for all this is, of course, Genesis 1:1. Failing to grasp the implications here will surely cause us to misunderstand some critical aspects of the nature of both God and His creation. Therefore, it behooves us to spend a little time thinking about the implications of Genesis 1:1.

On the basis of creation texts such as Genesis 1:1 and Proverbs 8:22-23, it can be argued that time, at least physical time, had a "beginning." In fact, Genesis 1:1, which is neither a subordinate clause nor a summary title, says, "In the beginning, God created the heavens and the earth." According to James Barr, this was an *absolute* beginning which, when taken with the expression, "So the evening and the morning were the first day" (verse 5), indicates this was, in fact, the very first day, which may well be intended to teach that "the beginning" was not just the beginning of the physical universe, but the beginning of time itself and that, therefore, God may be thought of as timeless.[14] In this statement, Barr appears to reflect what Jude said so succinctly: "To the only God our Saviour, through Jesus Christ our Lord, be glory, majesty, dominion and power, *before all time*, and now, and for evermore. Amen."[15] When this is coupled with Proverbs 8:22-23, which clearly looks back to "the beginning," it can be fairly said that the Old Testament implies that time started at the beginning. Add to this Jude's

---

[13] 2 Timothy 3:17.
[14] James Barr, *Biblical Words for Time*, 1962, pages 145-147.
[15] Jude 25, ASV of 1901.

statement mentioned above, along with John 1:1-3, which says: "In the beginning was the Word, and the Word was with God, and the Word was God. He was in the beginning with God. All things were made through Him, and without Him nothing was made that was made," and it seems clear that the Bible teaches the beginning of the creation was not just the beginning of space and matter, but it was the beginning of time as well.

If all this is true, and I think there is not much doubt about it, then the Creator, at least before He created, was neither subject to time (i.e., He was timeless) nor space. In addition, as the immortal and eternal God,[16] He did not, indeed He could not, consist of the material nature (matter) of His creation. He was, in fact, totally other (i.e., transcendent). All this stands in stark contrast with creation, which by virtue of its creation owes its existence to something outside itself (viz., God). It is in this regard that we are said to live, move and have our being in the Creator.[17] How, then, are some New Testament Christians able to claim that God is somehow limited by space or time?

It is only God, by virtue of who He is, who is free from the constraints of the space-time continuum. And it should be clear that the God who is not so free can never be anything more than one of the small "g" gods of orthotalksy. It is simply not possible that the one true God can be divided or torn asunder, and anyone who thinks so, no matter what position on the Holy Spirit he defends, is not honoring the God who has revealed Himself in the Scriptures. It is impossible for the omnipresent God to be "scattered...into thousands, perhaps millions, of fully functional, self-contained, independent units, each one the perfect clone of all

---

[16] See Deuteronomy 33:27; Romans 16:26; 1 Timothy 1:17.
[17] See Acts 17:28.

the others." In fact, the God who has revealed Himself in the Bible is a God who could make Himself known in a million simultaneous theophanies and still be present to all the rest of creation at the same time. He could indwell a multitude of Christians equally, and all at the same time, without diminishing Himself in the least. He can do all this not because He is *a* spirit, but because He is God, *the* uncreated Spirit, "the King eternal, immortal, invisible, the only wise God."[18]

Christians, particularly those who teach God's Word, must not transfer to God any of the creaturely limitations. As the Creator, He is simply not subject to them. Along these lines, it is interesting to me that modern science, which hasn't always been especially friendly to the Creator, has started to bow in His direction. Although I believe "big bang" cosmology to be inconsistent with the Biblical account of creation, and therefore wrong, nevertheless, it is most interesting to hear scientists conclude that time and space came into existence at "the beginning" of the universe. The British physicist, Paul Davies, typifies what I'm talking about:

> *If we extrapolate this prediction to its extreme, we reach a point when all distances in the universe have shrunk to zero. An initial cosmological singularity therefore forms a past temporal extremity to the universe. We cannot continue physical reasoning or even the concept of spacetime, through such an extremity. For this reason most cosmologists think of the initial singularity as the beginning of the universe. On this view the big bang repre-*

---

[18] See 1 Timothy 1:17; Jude 25.

sents the creation event, the creation not only of all the matter and energy of the universe, but also of spacetime itself.[19]

Others, addressing this same thing, assert: "At this singularity, space and time came into existence, literally nothing existed before the singularity, so, if the Universe originated as such a singularity, we would truly have a creation ex nihilo."[20]

This aspect of current cosmological theory is especially troubling for some scientists, particularly those with atheistic beliefs. For example, the Russian astrophysicist, Andrei Linde, acknowledges, rather candidly, the problem that such a model poses for him: "The most difficult aspect of this problem is not the existence of the singularity itself, but the question of what was *before* the singularity.... This problem lies somewhere at the boundary between physics and metaphysics."[21]

Sounds to me like Fred Hoyle's old "steady-state" theory (viz., an eternal universe) with its well-known dictum *Exnihilo, nihil fit* ("Out of nothing, nothing comes") has finally bitten the dust. As philosopher William Lane Craig says, "The steady state model has been abandoned by virtually everyone."[22]

So, the theory most scientists subscribe to today is the big bang model, especially the inflationary version. Again, I am not arguing that this theory is correct. In fact, I totally reject the 15 billion years this theory postulates for the universe. I mention it here

---

[19] "Spacetime Singularities in Cosmology and Black Hole Evaporations," in *The Study of Time III*, ed. J.T. Fraser, N. Lawrence, and D. Park, 1978, pages 78-79.

[20] John Barrow and Frank Tipler, *The Anthropic Cosmological Principle*, 1986, page 442.

[21] "The Inflationary Universe," *Reports on Progress in Physics* 47, 1984, page 976.

[22] *Reasonable Faith*, page 103.

because it argues that the expanding universe *necessarily* had a beginning, and that it did not begin to expand into already existing space, but that it was space itself—which prior to the big bang had not existed—that was expanding outwards, with the alleged cosmic expansion creating space as it went along.

Now, if scientists who are limited, in the things they do, to the material creation—although it is true they don't always act like they are—can understand the universe had a beginning, and that such a creation would have to be created *ex nihilo* or "out of nothing," then I should think that modern-day Christians who are, generally speaking, the best educated the world has ever known, should not fail to understand the profound implications of such a creation: namely, that the Creator is over and above time, space and all finite reality, and can no more be confined to space than He can be measured by time.

It is inescapable that if something exists now, one of three things must be true of it: (1) it is either eternal, (2) it is created by something that is eternal, or (3) it is self-created. The first option is ruled out by the Second Law of Thermodynamics, since an eternal universe would have wound down or dissipated a long time ago. The third clashes not only with the First Law of Thermodynamics, but with logic's Law of Contradiction, because in order to have created itself, the universe would have had to exist before it existed, an idea that is scientifically and philosophically ridiculous. This leaves only the second option, and the God extolled in this series satisfies all the necessary criteria of such a Creator. Natural revelation, when properly interpreted, points at a Being whose existence explains why science can explain anything, but why it cannot explain everything. As the famous and erudite Mr. Stephen Hawking has said about the big bang theory, "It would be difficult to explain why the universe should have begun in just this way, except as an act of God who intended to create beings like us."[23] Commenting on this, William Lane Craig wrote:

> *Since everything that began to exist has a cause of its existence, and since the universe began to exist, we conclude, therefore, that the universe has a cause of existence. We ought to ponder long and hard over this truly remarkable conclusion, for it means that transcending the entire universe there exists a cause which brought the universe into being ex nihilo.... This conclusion ought to stagger us, ought to fill us with a sense of awe and wonder at the knowledge that our whole universe was caused to exist by something beyond it and greater than it.*[24]

Finally, the high-profile astronomer, Robert Jastrow, Director of NASA's Goddard Institute for Space Studies, in an article in the *New York Times*, asked the question: "Have Astronomers Found God?" His answer was that they had, or had at least come close to doing so. After arguing that the universe had a beginning in time, and after accepting that its creation by an act of God was a reasonable possibility [Jastrow is a professed agnostic], he went on to point out that astronomical evidence points to a theistic view of the world: "The details differ, but the essential elements...are the same; the chain of events leading to man commenced suddenly and sharply at a definite moment in time, in a flash of light and energy."[25]

His final words in this article were quite appropriate to our study:

---

[23] *A Brief History of Time*, page 140.
[24] *The Kalam Cosmological Argument*, page 149.
[25] June 25, 1978.

This is an exceedingly strange development, unexpected by all but the theologians.... We scientists did not expect to find evidence for an abrupt beginning because we have had until recently such extraordinary success in tracing the chain of cause and effect backward in time.... At this moment it seems as though science will never be able to raise the curtain on the mystery of creation. For the scientist who has lived by his faith in the power of reason, the story ends like a bad dream. He has scaled the mountains of ignorance; he is about to conquer the highest peak; as he pulls himself over the final rock, he is greeted by a band of theologians who have been sitting there for centuries.[26]

Brethren, let us "act like men"[27] in the midst of a lost and dying world.[28] Let us determine to know and proclaim the Rock who is our salvation.[29] As we do so, let us forever put away from us the sham gods of orthotalksy.

---

[26] *Ibid.*
[27] 1 Corinthians 16:13.
[28] See Philippians 2:15.
[29] See 1 Corinthians 10:4; 1 Peter 2:7.

Chapter 10

The State: A Mortal, But Very Supreme, God

It is better to trust in the Lord than to put confidence in man. It is better to trust in the Lord than to put confidence in princes (Psalm 118:9). Do not put your trust in princes, nor in a son of man, in whom there is no hope (Psalm 146:3).

In Romans 13:1-7, we find a description of civil government as it is ordained by God. It is important to understand the apostle Paul is not saying that every government is ordained by God, as some have supposed. On the contrary, what he is telling us is precisely what type of government (viz., its character) God has ordained. If one understands this, then the difficulties Christians face in reconciling their obedience to God and the state are somewhat mitigated. For example, although many Christians believe that the teaching of the Bible demands they be obedient and supportive of both good and evil governments, no matter what the circumstances, this is not the teaching of Romans 13; nor do I believe it to be the teaching of other scriptures dealing with this subject.

The Bible teaches that the kind of rulers who have been ordained by God are not a "terror to good works, but to evil" (v. 3). They are described as "God's ministers" who have been ordained by Him for the good of those they govern. A part of that good is to "execute wrath on him who practices evil" (v. 4). Christians should be subject to civil government and its authorities not just because of their power to inflict punishment for wrongdoing, but because their consciences, properly instructed by God's Word, tell them that to do otherwise would be a violation of His Will. It is quite clear that God has ordained the higher powers and has placed responsibilities both on them and on those to whom they minister. If either the civil government or the citizens they govern conduct themselves contrary to the obligations and responsibilities God has placed upon them, then both lose their legitimacy in those matters.

Justice And Righteousness

Space does not permit me the room to cite the scriptural references, so I'll simply say what all Christians should know—namely, the Bible teaches all governments should be about the God-given tasks of doing justice and righteousness. In this regard, and although many have missed this point, Rome, although a pagan state, administered a system of civil justice that was amazingly equitable for its time.[1] This can be demonstrated from a study of some Biblical examples. For instance, when Jesus was on trial before Pilate, He was tried on a civil charge of fomenting insurrection[2] and was found not guilty.[3] He was put to death not because Roman civil justice demanded it, but because Pilate was a weak and corrupt public official who gave in to the Jews. Roman law and justice "proved" itself in its acquittal of Jesus. But Pontius Pilate "proved" himself by giving in to the Jews' threats, sending to His

---

[1] Mosheim, *Institutes of Ecclesiastical History, Ancient and Modern*, Book I, p. 2.
[2] See Luke 23:2.
[3] See Matthew 27:24.

death, as a result, one who was totally innocent of the charges against Him.[4]

When Paul was accused before Junuis Gallio Annaeus, the Roman proconsul of Achaia, his judgment was: "If it were a matter of wrongdoing or wicked crimes [i.e., a matter of civil law], O Jews, there would be reason why I should bear with you: But if it is a question of words and names, and your own law, look to it yourselves; for I do not want to be a judge of such matters."[5] In times past, this was the traditional position of the criminal and civil justice system in the United States. In fact, in 1871, the U.S. Supreme Court declared: "The law knows no heresy, and is committed to the support of no dogma, the establishment of no sect."[6]

When Paul's companions, Gaius and Aristarchus, were accused in an unlawful assembly, the town clerk informed the people that if they wanted to assemble to consider some religious matter, it would have to be done in a lawful assembly.[7] If, on the other hand, they had civil or criminal charges against any man, the law and its deputies were available to them.[8]

Again, when Paul was wrongfully charged by the Jews with being "a creator of dissension among all the Jews throughout the world, and a ringleader of the sect of the Nazarenes," and one "who has even tried to profane the temple," and would have been killed by the Jews, he was saved by Roman law and justice. Although it is true that Felix, the Judean procurator, was corrupt and held Paul for two years when he should have been released, hoping

---

[4] See John 19:12.
[5] Acts 18:14-15.
[6] *Watson v. Jones*, 13 Wall [U.S.] 679.
[7] See Acts 19:39.
[8] See Acts 19:38.

"that money would be given him by Paul,"[9] nevertheless, the Jews were unable to kill him due to the protection offered by Roman law. When Festus took over as governor from Felix and would have returned Paul to Jerusalem to stand trial, Paul was able to exercise a right provided under Roman law and appealed his case to Caesar.[10] Even though Festus thought Paul to be mad, he judged him guiltless of any wrongdoing[11] and would have set him free except for the fact he had made his appeal to Caesar.

At the time Jesus gave His instructions to His disciples concerning their responsibilities to civil government, we know there was a system of law and order practiced by Rome that, although flawed, was still beneficial to those it governed. And even though Augustus (63 B.C. - A.D. 14) had done much to revive the ancient cults of the Romans, the Jews and, later, the Christians, who were considered by the Romans to be a sect of the Jews, were exempted from emperor worship. Even though it is true that in A.D. 64, after the burning of Rome, the Roman government, under Nero, made the practice of Christianity a criminal offense, it is also true that after Nero's suicide four years later, Christians were given a somewhat lengthy respite from persecution. Therefore, it can be seen that the general domestic tranquility provided by *pax Romana* was both beneficial and worthy of support.

Government Ordained By Satan

In contrast to the God-ordained government of Romans 13, there is the Satan-ordained government of Revelation 13. In the

---

[9] Acts 24:26.
[10] See Acts 25:11.
[11] See Acts 25:25.

latter instance, it was still the Roman government; but something very frightening had taken place. In just a few short years, Rome had gone from a government that offered protection for those doing good and punishment for those doing evil, to a government that protected the criminal and punished the law-abiding. I think it's a good possibility the "mystery of iniquity" mentioned in 2 Thessalonians 2:7 might have had to do with the transition that was already at work, but not yet accomplished, in the Roman government at the time Paul wrote his second letter to the Thessalonians. Nero became emperor of Rome in A.D. 54, the same year Paul is believed to have written 2 Thessalonians. Nero, who is alleged to have committed suicide in A.D. 68, was described by Tertullian, in his *Apology*, as "the first emperor who dyed his sword in Christian blood." Anyone familiar with the terribly perverse life of this man who murdered his own mother, who had been declared a god by the Roman Senate, and who was the first to bring the unjust wrath of the Roman government against the Christians, would have very little trouble seeing Nero as a part of "the mystery of iniquity."

The Sea Beast

I believe the sea beast of Revelation 13 represents the civil and military powers of the Roman government as it was used by the emperors and other authorities for evil instead of good. God never ordained civil government to be a "terror to good works"; therefore, any government engaged in such activities has come under the influence of Satan. As a matter of fact, this is exactly the teaching of Revelation 13:2, where it is learned that the sea beast was given his power, his throne, and his great authority by "the dragon." According to verse three, this illegitimate power received a "deadly [i.e., a mortal] wound" that would later be healed. It is my opinion that the suicide of the tyrant Nero represented this "deadly wound." After Nero, the next three emperors (Galba, Otho, and Vitellius), all installed by the Praetorian Guard, came and went in quick fashion. In fact, they were so busy trying to keep from being killed, they had no time to even think about persecuting Christians. There is no record that the next two emperors (Vespasian, A.D. 69-79, and Titus, A.D. 79-81) ever used their authority to persecute Christians. Christians were not again openly harassed until the reign of Domitian (A.D. 81-96).

It was during Domitian's reign that the "deadly wound was healed." According to the historian Eusebius, Domitian was Nero's successor as persecutor of the church. About him he wrote:

Domitian, indeed, having exercised his cruelty against many, and unjustly slain no small number of noble and illustrious men at Rome, and having, without cause, punished vast numbers of honorable men with exile and the confiscation of their property, at length established himself as the successor of Nero, in his hatred and hostility toward God. He was the second that raised a persecution against us, although his father Vespasian had attempted nothing to our prejudice.[12]

Furthermore, it must not go unnoticed that Tertullian identified Domitian as "a limb [viz., an extension or continuation] of the bloody Nero."[13]

---

[12] *Ecclesiastical History*, Book II, Chapter XVII.
[13] *Apology*, Chapter V.

The Earth Beast

Then there is the earth beast of Revelation 13:11. It represents, I think, the perverted religion of the Romans which required citizens of the state to engage in Caesar-worship. This earth beast is twice referred to as the "false prophet."[14] The Concilia (i.e., the contingent of state priests) had the responsibility of promoting Caesar-worship and, deriving their authority from the civil and military powers of Rome,[15] forced all citizens to acknowledge Caesar as *dominus et deus,* which means "my Lord and God." That which had been instituted by Augustus (viz., the divinity of the emperor) was fully revived in the tyrant Nero and, after a short reprieve, was resurrected in Domitian.[16] Under such a system, Christians who would not acknowledge the Roman gods, including the emperor, were referred to, ironically, as "atheists." As such, they continued to be officially persecuted until A.D. 311.

666, The Number Of A Man

Contrary to what many think, "666," although it is definitely referred to as "the number of the beast" in Revelation 13:18, is not really the identifying mark of the beast itself. Instead, 666 is the "number of a man," and is used, I think, to identify those who bow down to the state and its ministers as if they were gods. This could be called Babelism or Statism. All who promote or engage in such activities make themselves enemies of the only True and Living God and are, without repentance, destined for everlasting

---

[14] See Revelation 16:13 and 19:20.
[15] See Revelation 13:12.
[16] Consider Revelation 13:14.

destruction. The "mark of the beast" seems to have been the *certificate* or *license* to engage in the benefits of Roman citizenship. To honor the Roman gods and to acknowledge Caesar as divine were deemed acts *essential* to good citizenship, and all that was usually required of the Christians was for them to buy a little incense from the Concilia and burn it to Caesar as god. The Roman authorities made it clear that they did not have to stop being a Christian in order to do so. In other words, just burn a little incense today and tomorrow you can continue to worship Christ. For many, the temptation was too great, as burning a pinch of incense made the difference as to whether or not one was allowed to work in the trade guilds. No pinch of incense, no job. It was as simple as that.

Modern Incense Burners

I believe there are Christians today who are burning a little incense to Caesar, bowing to the state in matters in which the state has no legitimate, God-given authority. For example, after participating in a forum on whether or not a Christian could be involved in carnal warfare, I was approached by a brother who explained to me rather energetically that he believed a Christian was under obligation to fight in any war his government became involved in. This, he exclaimed, was exactly what the Bible taught on the subject in Matthew 22:21, Romans 13:1-7, Titus 3:1, and 1 Peter 2:13-14. Whether this brother actually knew better and was simply trying to rationalize his predilections, or whether he was just plain ignorant of God's Word, I had no way of knowing. Either will ultimately lead to a rejection of God and participation in conduct that is sinful. But here's my point: when a Christian says he must *always* obey the government, then what he is ultimately saying, whether he realizes it or not, is that he will recognize no power above that of the state. In other words, and he would, of course, deny it, the state has become, in point of fact, his god (i.e., he has received the "mark of the beast").

Although it comes as a shock to many Christians, idolatry did not cease to exist with the completion of the New Testament. Babelism or Statism (viz., man's effort to deify the state) is very much alive today. This is further demonstrated by a school teacher who wrote in one of the popular religious magazines among us in the 1980s about the "near panic" she believed prevailed in the minds of some preachers concerning the public schools and humanism. Although very critical of such an attitude, she went on to accurately identify some of the techniques used by the public schools to inculcate humanistic philosophy (viz., role playing, values clarification sessions, situation ethics, *et cetera*). She tried to justify all of this by saying: "The laws of our land, fearing interference with the parents' right to teach their children religious beliefs and/or values, forbids the teaching of moral decisions based on God or the Bible, so the teacher *must* teach these decisions based on man and his limits and consequences, in relation to other members of society." Her reason for believing it *"must"* be done this way was—perhaps you've already guessed it—Romans 13:1-7. In other words, this Christian believed that she must teach her students the anti-God, anti-Christian, anti-Biblical philosophies of Humanism because this is what the state had commanded her to do; and she, after all, must obey the state because the Bible tells her to do so.

Here we have, in my opinion, a Christian who has received the mark of the beast and doesn't seem to know it. She may just be ignorant of God's word, and this would be bad enough. However, it could be that she is simply trying to rationalize the type of behavior the government has forced upon her in recent years. But here's my point: this school teacher, who was bought with the precious blood of Jesus Christ, did not seem to understand the implications of Acts 4:18-19 and 5:29. These passages clearly teach there are circumstances in which the Christian *must disobey* civil authorities. In fact, the knowledgeable student of the Bible ought to know that when the authorities command a Christian to do those things that are contrary to the Word of God, he or she *must* be disobedient to those authorities.

Perhaps you realize that the brother and sister mentioned above are in error. Maybe you even agree with me they have received the mark of the beast. But permit me to turn your attention to some areas where many of us could be just as guilty, but not know it.

In Matthew 28:18, Jesus said, "All authority has been given to Me in heaven and on earth." With His all-encompassing authority firmly established in the minds of those to whom He spoke, Jesus instructed them to "Go, therefore, and make disciples of all nations, baptizing them in the name of the Father and of the Son and of the Holy Spirit" (v. 19). By this, we necessarily infer the gospel is to have free course in the world, regardless of the restrictions governments attempt to place on it. But if we truly believed and practiced this doctrine, then there would more than likely be at least a few of us occupying the prisons and gulags of those nations in the world that are antagonistic toward Christianity.

When governments tell us we cannot preach the gospel of Jesus Christ within their borders, too many of us obediently obey. When they forbid the importation of Bibles, too many of us dutifully comply. This is all done under the guise of obeying the laws of the land. But what the church really needs today are men and women who are willing to be criminals, when necessary, for the cause of Christ. And make no mistake about it, as soon as we refuse to obey governmental authorities for the sake of Jesus Christ, we will immediately be branded as criminals. For sure, smuggling Bibles into countries that prohibit the printing or importation of such will be identified as a criminal act. However, such would not be a sin according to Scripture. In fact, we are engaged in wickedness when we are willing to obey such governments in these matters.

Some understand this and have broken such laws when necessary. But it is very difficult to think about such disobedience while living within those governments that have not been openly antagonistic toward Christianity. In fact, such a concept is very difficult for most of us. Nevertheless, Western governments, including our own, are becoming increasingly hostile to New Testament Christianity. Consequently, it may be time to think seriously about our Christian obligation to engage in holy disobedience even here in the United States of America.

Recent Examples Of The Government's Mounting Hostility

One example of our country's becoming increasingly hostile to New Testament Christianity can be seen in the 1989 Oklahoma court case involving the Collinsville church of Christ and a withdrawn-from fornicator. In that case, the courts ruled that the Collinsville church broke the law when doing what the Bible clearly says they *must* do. The church, directed by the elders, was in the process of withdrawing from an accused fornicator when she "withdrew" her membership. (I know some brethren argue that we can't withdraw from the withdrawn, but most brethren believe the local church can and must withdraw from such in order to remain faithful to the Lord.) The Collinsville church ultimately withdrew from the accused fornicator (who incidentally did not deny that she had engaged in fornication, only that it was none of the church's business what she did). She sued them for defaming her character in the community and the church lost. As a result, the court directed the church to pay the withdrawn-from

The Christian & Idolatry

fornicator $390,000 ($205,000 in actual damages and $185,000 in punitive damages) plus $44,737 in prejudgment interest.[17]

Subsequently, a church in California lost a similar case and was ordered to pay a ridiculous amount. As you can imagine, this all had a very chilling effect on church discipline. Now, a heretofore minority position held by brethren that says you can't withdraw from the withdrawn has court precedent to back up its claim. How many elderships, fearing the results mentioned above, have thought it prudent to just go ahead and burn a little incense to Caesar rather than do what it is the Lord has commanded them to do, I do not know. But that times have changed should be obvious to us all.

Unfortunately, our government has begun to exhibit the telling signs of a transition from a Romans 13 government ordained by God to a Revelation 13 regime under the influence of Satan. But please, don't misunderstand me; I do not believe the United States government is a Revelation 13 type government. Nevertheless, there definitely seems to be a "mystery of iniquity" at work in its midst.

It is disturbing to me that so many Christians seem to be so unaware of what is actually occurring in our day. Many New Testament Christians associate being a good Christian with being a good American. However, this is simply not true.

Yes, in times past, because of the principle of government "under God" this country was founded on, being both a good Christian and a good American were easier than they are today. However, I am not saying that even those years were without controversy, for any time a Christian is trying to live consistent with

---

[17] *Guinn v. Church of Christ of Collinsville*, 775 P.2d 766 [Okla. 1989].

the truths taught in the Bible there will be difficulties both with society and government. But it can no longer be denied that civil disobedience, long ignored by Christians living in America, will become an increasingly important subject as this country continues to sever itself from the Biblical base that has served it so well throughout the years.

The God That Has Clearly Failed

For those of us living in the twenty-first century, the fairly modern development of the nation-state has become so pervasive, its vast powers so "normal," and our dependence on it so all-encompassing, that anything that attempts to severely limit its powers seems "old hat" or antiquated, even when such is, unfortunately, the Constitution of the United States. Although lip service continues to be given to the Constitution, in truth, its safeguards, which clearly and severely restricted the exercise of government, have been largely abandoned in our time.

In his 1948 book, *Ideas Have Consequences*, reflecting the sentiment often attributed to Oswald Spengler, Richard M. Weaver wrote that "Civilization has been an intermittent phenomenon; to this truth we have allowed ourselves to be blinded by the insolence of material success."[18] Indeed, ideas do have consequences. Not because Oswald Spengler said so, but because this is what the Bible says and experience has taught us.[19]

For example, if secular humanism is right when it claims no God will save us—namely, that we must, in fact, save ourselves—then the nation-state, a fairly recent invention of man,

---

[18] In the introduction to the reprint edition, September 15, 1984, p. 17.

[19] Consider Proverbs 23:7a.

becomes the human race's only hope of salvation. Of course, the salvation being sought by such thinking is not the so-called "pie in the sky by and by" that Christianity is purported to promise. It is, instead, the earthly comforts of materialism—something John Humphries (my good friend, fellow gospel preacher, and long-time missionary to India) has dubbed, "soup, soap, salve, sex, and social security."

In Romans 1:18-32, the inspired writer outlined the sad scenario that has become so commonplace in the history of mankind:

- A nation rejects God,

- it turns to false religion,

- it becomes bogged down in immorality and violence,

- and then God judges it.

That this is the slippery slope which this nation is now traveling seems hard to deny. This means that without national repentance, God's judgment will surely come upon this nation. If not, then it might well be deemed appropriate by some to argue that the Lord, in fact, owes Sodom and Gomorrah an apology. As a matter of fact, and I hate to even think about it, perhaps the events taking place in our time indicate that such judgment has already begun.

Someone might say, "But we are the most powerful country on the face of the earth, the only remaining superpower." Yes, this is no doubt true, but when God judges this nation, it would not surprise me for Him to do so when it is at the height of its political and military power. In other words, as much as I thought of Ronald Reagan and his so-called "cowboy" mentality, and regardless of how much an integral part I believe he played in the fall of the U.S.S.R., a government he dubbed "the evil empire," there remains little doubt in my mind that it was actually God who took that evil nation down in such a dramatic and unexpected way and time. Likewise, without genuine repentance, and when the time is right, the Lord will take this nation down, as well. This grieves me first of all because I have children and grandchildren who will be affected by the consequences of such judgment. Second, it doesn't have to be this way. America, a nation founded on principles taught in God's word, does not have to forget God, but in so many cases it has.

In Psalm 11:3, the question is asked, "If the foundations be destroyed, what can the righteous do?" Of course, when the foundations are destroyed the righteous are made a prey of the wicked. Consequently, the very purpose of government is the protection of the righteous or law abiding. Government, as ordained by God, is a mechanical remedy against evil.[20] Thomas Jefferson clearly understood this principle, and so must we if we are to keep the "unalienable rights" endowed us by "our Creator." Jesus Christ is sovereign of the universe. Thus, His law is above all laws and all men everywhere are subject to His authority. Many earthly authorities have not understood this. As a result, they have not heeded the wise counsel of the psalmist, who said: "Serve the Lord with fear, and rejoice with trembling. Kiss the Son, lest He be angry, and you perish in the way."[21] Indeed, let the men and women of America, and all nations, soberly reflect upon the eminent admonition of Proverbs 14:34, which says, "Righteousness exalts a nation, but sin is a reproach to any people."

---

[20] See Romans 13:1-7.
[21] Psalm 2:11-12.

Idolatry Defined

Idolatry—whether it be what we normally think of as the regular pagan kind, or whether it be the kind that seeks to deify the state—is aptly described by the apostle Paul in Romans 1:20b-23, where he says that man is without excuse, because,...

> *although they knew God, they did not glorify Him as God, nor were thankful, but became futile in their thoughts, and their foolish hearts were darkened. Professing themselves to be wise, they became fools, and changed the glory of the incorruptible God into an image made like corruptible man—and birds and four-footed beasts and creeping things.*

He went on to say in verse 25 that these are the kind of people who "exchanged the truth of God for the lie, and worshiped and served the creature, rather than the Creator." He concluded with this:

> *For this reason God gave them up to vile passions. For even their women exchanged the natural use for what is against nature. Likewise also the men, leaving the natural use of the woman, burned in their lust for one another, men with men committing what is shameful, and receiving in themselves the penalty of their error which was due. And even as they did not like to retain God in their knowledge, God gave them over to a debased mind, to do those things which are not fitting; being filled with all unrighteousness, sexual immorality, wickedness, covetousness, maliciousness; full of envy, murder, strife, deceit, evil-mindedness; they are whisperers, backbiters, haters of God, violent, proud, boasters, inventors of evil things, disobedient to parents, undiscerning, untrustworthy, unloving, unforgiving, unmerciful; who knowing the righteous judgment of God, that*

those who practice such things are worthy of death, not only do the same but also approve of those who practice them.

This is a very accurate description of our nation today and, without national repentance, God's judgment will come, if it hasn't already started.

Yes, ideas do have consequences, and as the collective mind of a nation thinks, so is it. Statism instructs its captivated followers to look to the state to supply all its needs. However, as Joel Belz pointed out in a perceptive article in the September 17, 2005 edition of *World Magazine*, the false god of government cannot satisfy in times of plenty or want. Commenting about the almost universal dissatisfaction with the government's Katrina response, Belz said in part:

> *Happiness with the result of any big government effort, of course, is almost an oxymoron. The reason is simply that when people start putting their trust in big government, they've attached themselves to a false god. And false gods can't produce the goods.*
>
> *What we saw in New Orleans last week was the pathetic picture of people whose expectations in a false god had been so enhanced that when the false god stumbled for a day or two, some of his worshippers flew into a rage. They'd been betrayed, they said. Not only had their god failed to tend their obvious physical needs in prompt style; he had made them look weak and foolish in the process.*
>
> *...*
>
> *And then remember this: That such a people will in the days to come develop a bigger and bigger appetite for gods who promise them everything. And then they will show a lower and lower tolerance for gods who do not perform.*

The Christian & Idolatry

He went on to say:

The smug pretense—exhibited over the last few days by politicians, by media writers and broadcasters, by religious leaders, and by entertainers—claimed repeatedly that if government had just been prepared, much of the horror left by Hurricane Katrina might have been precluded. But the suggestion is false on its face, for it is difficult to conceive of any organization of human capacities that might have tended to the needs of half a million people much better than what you've watched since Aug. 30. News reports have suggested repeatedly that even in the Third World, things would have gone faster than they did in the Gulf states. Don't believe it. In the Third World, hunger is perpetual. What you saw for a week or two was painful, but exceptional. What you see so many other places is chronic.

According to the Bible, deliberately shortchanging the poor, or even carelessly ignoring their needs, is wicked behavior. But raising false expectations is also a cruel game. And that includes constantly dividing the people and feeding the illusion that if we'd just had some other president, or some other governor, or some other mayor, we could all be content. If government can't make us happy even when there isn't an emergency, why should we make it our god when the next Katrina comes blowing through?

Sadly, what many saw happening in the aftermath of Katrina was colored by racism. But it had very little, I think, to do with the differences between blacks and whites. Instead, it was the result of the various "isms" that plague not just New Orleans, but all of America. These are Narcissism, Hedonism, Materialism, and Pluralism, to name but a few of the major culprits. These isms have been spawned by the rampant secularism that has swept our nation. It will do us good to spend a little time defining and thinking about the ramifications of these doctrines and how it applies to what we saw in New Orleans and the rest of our nation in the aftermath of Katrina.

Narcissism

Narcissism says, "Me first." It says, "I'm number one." The narcissist is in love with himself. Other people matter only as they serve to fulfill and satisfy him. He is only concerned about his rights, his privileges and his happiness. Wives, husbands, children, employers, employees and fellow citizens all take a second seat to the narcissist. He is a "me, my, mine" kind of person.[22] He is in love with the self-esteem, self-love, pull-your-own-strings, put-yourself-first, you're-number-one shibboleths of modern-day pop-psychology. When one becomes infected with this spiritual disease, he begins to talk about doing something for himself. He talks of being tired of doing what God, and everyone else, wants him to do. If the one infected happens to be a Christian, He begins to complain about the sermons not being uplifting enough. He protests that Bible classes just aren't positive enough. He whines about the worship services of the local congregation just not doing anything for him anymore. It is not long before families, church unity, ethics in the marketplace, and community stability begin to play second fiddle to the "star" of the show—Numero Uno! By contrast, the Jesus of the cross instructs us to crucify self as we

---

[22] See Luke 12:16-21.

learn to put others first.[23] He teaches us to give ourselves away to God and others.[24]

Hedonism

Closely related to narcissism, hedonism says that life ought to be lived solely for pleasure. It is personified in the Playboy philosophy of the 1950s and '60s, and is summed up in the motto, "If it feels good, do it." It fans the flames of pornography and homosexuality as it promotes anything and everything that supposedly gives "pleasure." It replaces responsible living with a "thrill at any cost" approach to life. It is responsible for the proliferation of sexually transmitted diseases, including AIDS. Those given over to hedonism are addicted to lust and can never be satisfied and, in their attempts to satisfy their insatiable appetites, hedonists frequently become quite promiscuous. This, of course, destroys many marriages and homes. Finally, the pursuit of pleasure at any cost leaves men and women broken, lonely, and sad. On the other hand, those who follow God's Word will find happiness and satisfaction in the "one flesh" relationship ordained by God, and will know ultimate contentment in pleasing Christ, not themselves.[25]

Materialism

Materialism says, "I am what I have" and "He who dies with the most toys wins." Instead of concentrating on spiritual and eternal things, materialism seeks after those things that can be seen,

---

[23] See Matthew 16:24,25; Philippians 2:3.
[24] See Matthew 22:34-40.
[25] See 2 Corinthians 5:9.

touched, tasted, smelled, and possessed. Everything, and everybody, takes a second seat to materialism—the accumulation of things. As a result, such fall into temptation and a snare, and into many foolish and harmful lusts which drown them in destruction and perdition.[26] In contrast to this, Christianity teaches that we ought to be laying up for ourselves treasures in heaven. In other words, life is an investment, and we can either invest for short-term benefits or long-term gains.

Pluralism

Modern America prides itself in its pluralism. Pluralism is modern culture's belief that there are many different "right ways" to live and believe. It says:

> *Find whatever works for you. If it's Jesus and Christianity, fine. If it's Hinduism, great. Whatever you want to believe is just fine. Find the church of your choice. Dogmatism is out. Absolutes are out. All paths lead to the same God. God wouldn't turn away sincere people.*

This then is what pluralism is. In a pluralistic America, even witchcraft and Devil worship are constitutionally protected religions. Many Americans today act like they think the Creator of the universe is somehow limited by the Constitution of the United States. He is not! Jesus emphatically said: "I am the way, the truth, and the life. No one comes to the Father except through Me."[27] The apostle Paul unequivocally taught, "Nor is there salvation in

---

[26] See 1 Timothy 6:9-10.
[27] John 14:6.

any other, for there is no other name under heaven given among men by which we must be saved."[28]

It should not be thought ironic that New Orleans prides itself as being the personification of all these isms. Was Katrina God's judgment on New Orleans for its flaunted and much advertised debauchery? It very well could have been. But this is what I do know: any city, culture, or society totally given over to pluralism has forgotten that there is a Law above the law. Consequently, these will honor God and be blessed, or they will continue to disobey God and pay the bitter consequences. If not now, then eventually.

But to suggest that Katrina or even the events of September 11th might have been a wake-up call for America to repent has been met with the severest of condemnations. Yet, a nation that has permitted the killing of over a million unborn babies a year since 1973, legalized witchcraft and Devil worship, and promotes and protects alternative lifestyles (viz., homosexuality, lesbianism, *et cetera*) is certainly due some sort of judgment.

Instead of bowing down to Caesar as if he were god and burning their little pinch of incense, Christians must honor no God but God. We will gladly do so, or we will perish.

---

[28] Acts 4:12.

Chapter 11

Scientism: Modernity's Sacred Cow

Beware lest anyone cheat you through philosophy and empty deceit, according to the tradition of men, according to the basic principles of the world, and not according to Christ (Colossians 2:8).

In this chapter, we're going to be talking about something Francis Schaeffer called "modern, modern science."[1] But in order to do so, I want to remind you all that there are no true "unbelievers." As G. K. Chesterton once commented, "When people stop believing in God, they don't believe in nothing, they believe in everything."[2] And so, the god that has captured the hearts and minds of modernity—although it started well and somewhat less than deity some three hundred years ago—is Almighty Science. Enshrined on the altar of this sacred cow is something known as "the scientific method." Bowing to this god, Bertrand Russell said, "Whatever knowledge is attainable must be attained by scientific means; and what science cannot discover, mankind cannot know."[3]

---

[1] *The Church At The End Of The Twentieth Century*, page 16.
[2] Quoted by John Blanchard, *Does God Believe In Atheists*, 2000, page 338.
[3] *Religion And Science*, page 243.

This kind of thinking—the kind that makes a virtual deity of science—is popularly dubbed "Scientism," a man-made think-so that says science *alone* is the only rational approach to securing truth in the world. For those who bow at its totems and worship at its altar, the Bible is nothing more than an out-dated book with no real significance for twenty-first-century man. One of its high priests, Isaac Asimov, said, "The Bible describes a Universe created by God, maintained by him and instantly and constantly directed by him, while science describes a Universe in which it is not necessary to postulate the existence of God at all."[4] In a 1998 debate at Oxford University entitled "God—For or Against?," which was broadcast on England's T.V., Channel 4, Peter Atkins, an atheist and lecturer in Physics at the University, chided the audience to:

Use your brains—the most wonderful in the universe—and through your brains you will find you do not need God. There is no necessity for God because science can explain everything.

For those who think this way, the sacred cow of science is invested with *omnipotence* (giving us increasing control over nature), *omniscience* (knowing all the answers) and *infallibility* (telling us the claims of science are beyond dispute). Consequently, we are now expected to genuflect before any sentence that begins with "Science proves...."

That we live in a time where "God says..." has been replaced by "Science says..." is clear and obvious. Over a century ago, philosopher J. W. Draper, in his book, *History of the Conflict Between Religion and Science*, predicted, "The time approaches when we must make the choice between a quiescent Faith and ever-advancing Science, between faith with its medieval consolations and Science

---

[4] *In The Beginning*, page 13.

whose triumphs are sound and enduring."[5] In 1997, making the point that we now live in such a time, Richard Lewontin, a Harvard geneticist, voiced the following:

Our willingness to accept scientific claims that are against common sense is the key to an understanding of the real struggle between science and the supernatural. We take the side of science in spite of the patent absurdity of some of its constructs...in spite of the tolerance of the scientific community for unsubstantiated just-so stories, because we have [an] a priori *commitment...to materialism. It is not that the methods and institutions of science somehow compel us to accept a material explanation of the phenomenal world but, on the contrary, that we are forced by our* a priori *adherence to material causes to create an apparatus of investigation and a set of concepts that produce material explanations, no matter how counter-intuitive, no matter how mystifying to the uninitiated. Moreover that materialism is absolute for we cannot allow a Divine foot in the door.*[6]

The *a priori*[7] materialism of which Lewontin wrote caused the late Stephen Jay Gould, Professor of Geology and Paleontology at Harvard University and President of the American Association for the Advancement of Science, to remark:

We are here because one odd group of fishes had a peculiar fin anatomy that could transform into legs for terrestrial creatures; because comets struck the earth and wiped out dinosaurs, thereby

---

[5] Reported in *The Sunday Telegraph*, February 28, 1999.
[6] *New York Review of Books*, January 9, 1997.
[7] A Latin term meaning without reference to experience or fact. Frequently, such thinking is reflected in those who already have their minds made up about something or the other.

> *giving mammals a chance not otherwise available (so thank your lucky stars in a literal sense); because the earth never froze entirely during an ice age; because a small and tenuous species, arising in Africa a quarter of a million years ago, has managed, so far, to survive by hook and crook. We may yearn for a "higher" answer—but none exists.*[8]

And how did professor Gould purport to know all this? Well, omnipotent, omniscient Science, of course. It is interesting that those who believe that science, in its omniscience, can answer every question, cannot even give an answer for the very thing that makes science effective in the first place—natural laws! Science can be practiced only because the universe is controlled by natural laws, but actual science, by definition, cannot account for the laws' existence or origin.

It can produce theories as to what happened in the first moments of the universe, claiming, in some instances to take us back to "planck time" (a tiny fraction of a second after the alleged big bang), but it cannot go back beyond the "zero time point." As Edward Andrews, Emeritus Professor of Materials Science at the University of London, has said, "Thus it follows that science, even at its most speculative, must of necessity stop short of offering any explanation or even description of the actual event of origin."[9] In other words, science can *speculate* as to how the world came into being, but it cannot explain why it should have done so. Therefore, "Why does the world exist?" must forever remain a basic and fundamental mystery for science.

I am glad that Gould and Asimov, both of whom recently passed from this life, lived long enough to see their audaciously

---

[8] Cited by Ravi Zacharias, *Can Man Live Without God?*, page 31.
[9] *God, Science and Evolution*, page 35.

arrogant claims for Almighty Science evaporate before their very eyes. As I pointed out in the last chapter, a consensus has arisen in the scientific community that the space-time continuum which defines our universe had a beginning. This idea, which is a claim the Bible made a long, long time ago, destroys the premises of materialism/naturalism on which both Asimov and Gould made their faith-based claims, and overthrows, practically single-handedly, most of the previously held scientific ideas about the universe.

Before going any further, let me make it clear that I am not, nor have I ever been, anti-science. Modern science is very good and beneficial. However, if science is not to be deified, it must know its limitations, as it is obvious that a god with limitations is no God at all. In truth, modern science, and those who practice it, must admit ignorance about many, many things. Commenting on this, quantum theory expert Erwin Schrödinger wrote:

> *I am very astonished that the scientific picture of the real world around me is very deficient. It gives a lot of factual information, puts all our experiences in a magnificently consistent order, but it is ghastly silent about all and sundry that is really near to our hearts...it knows nothing of beautiful and ugly, good or bad, God and eternity. Science sometimes pretends to answer questions in these domains, but the answers are very often so silly that we are not inclined to take them seriously.*[10]

This, it seems to me, is an extremely wise attitude. On the other hand, those who claim their sacred cow can explain everything (or that is *capable* of explaining everything) overlook the fact that science cannot even explain itself. Yes, it can explain many things in

---

[10] Schrödinger, *Nature and the Greeks*, cited in Wilkinson, *Thinking Clearly About God and Science*, page 67.

the natural/material world, and this is unquestionably its strength, but it can only do so in terms of natural law, which the scientist in turn accepts as a "given" without being able to explain how or why it exists. In other words, science can tell us a great deal about our physical make-up, but it cannot tell us *how* the mind of man functions. In fact, it cannot even tell us *why* the mind should exist at all.

There is nothing wrong with modern science. It has been, and will continue to be, of great benefit to mankind. But it is that "modern, modern science" of which Francis Schaeffer wrote that is the problem. Science is not a thing (or an *it*, if you will). It has no essential existence of its own, but is an enterprise (not an entity), a way of learning by observation and experiment. As such, science is a servant (or a tool) to man's insatiable appetite for knowledge, and it should be remembered that in ancient times "science" was synonymous with "knowledge." But "modern, modern science" has made this endeavor a "God-free zone" and, in doing so, has created the monster called "Scientism." Now, the servant demands not only obedience, but obeisance as well.

Scientism And The Battle For The Public School System

In a far-reaching and, I think, terribly-flawed definition of science, the late Judge William R. Overton, in the famous creation science trial in Little Rock, Arkansas, in December 1981, wrote:

> *More precisely, the essential characteristics of science are 1) It is guided by natural law; 2) It has to be explanatory by reference to natural law; 3) It is testable against the empirical world; 4) Its*

conclusions are tentative, i.e., are not necessarily the final word; and 5) It is falsifiable.[11]

This ruling, although objected to even by some evolutionists, effectively articulates the official position as to what constitutes true science, and it doesn't take a mental heavyweight to figure out that Judge Overton wasn't talking about science being neutral or agnostic. In fact, it's not hard to figure out that Judge Overton wasn't even talking about methodological naturalism. In rendering his decision, the judge made it obviously clear that he had imbibed philosophical naturalism and was, in turn, imposing its assumptions (namely, scientific naturalism) on the doing of science.

Judge Overton was under obligation to be absolutely neutral, but notice that his decision starts by saying that something is science only if it focuses on the natural world, is guided by natural law, and/or explains by reference to natural law. So, let's break this down into three different claims and consider first the phrase "guided by natural law." What does this mean? If it means "seeks to explain in terms of natural law," then this second phrase reduces to the third one (i.e., "explains by reference to natural law"), and we will consider this a bit later. Perhaps guided by natural law means "motivated by a desire to find a natural explanation." If so, then this is clearly not a necessary or sufficient condition for something to count as science.

For example, a philosopher, who is not a theist, may be motivated to find a natural (i.e., a nonsupernatural) explanation for the existence and nature of morality, but in doing so, he is not doing science. On the other hand, a large number of men in the history

---

[11] Cited in Norman L. Geisler, *The Creator in the Courtroom*, 1982, page 176.

of science did science from a motivation to please God and think His thoughts after Him. Some of these practiced science with the firm belief that no natural explanation of a particular phenomenon was available. A good example of this is to be found in the great botanist, Carl Linnaeus, who founded modern taxonomy in 1735 with his work *Systema Naturae*. Linnaeus, unless someone wants to engage in an undocumented case of revisionist history, was a creationist who was motivated by his belief that no natural explanation was available for the existence and nature of living organisms. Even so, who can effectively argue that his work was not science?

It should be clear, then, that people can have a variety of reasons for carrying on their scientific endeavors, and their private motivations and convictions are not particularly relevant in assessing the question of whether their work and theories are really scientific. This is true, of course, only if science is really agnostic or neutral. But instead of science truly being neutral, the current priesthood of scientism demands that all practitioners of the craft bow in deference to the totem of philosophical (metaphysical) naturalism, which says the physical/material world is all there is. In other words, when all is said and done and the battle finally gets underway, the scientific scabbards fall away to reveal ideological swords.

Therefore, it ought to be clear to all that Judge Overton's definition in the McClean opinion was clearly and terribly flawed. If it were being applied today with any degree of fairness (it is only being applied to creationism), it would prohibit Darwinism, just like it does creationism, from being taught in the classrooms of America. Even so, most leading scientists dogmatically insist that the molecules-to-man evolution be taught as a fact to the exclusion of all other postulates (viz., creationism). It makes no difference that evolution in this broad sense (viz., macroevolution) is unproven and unprovable, and thus cannot reasonably be considered a fact.

It is clearly not subject to testing by the ordinary methods of experimental science. Therefore, it does not, in a strict sense, even qualify as a scientific theory. It is a postulate and may serve as a model within which attempts may be made to explain and correlate the evidence from the historical record (i.e., the fossil record) and to make predictions concerning the nature of future discoveries.

Evolutionists, however, insist that evolution is fact, not theory. Philosopher Tom Bethell describes the true situation when he states:

Evolution is perhaps the most jealously guarded dogma of the American public philosophy. Any sign of serious resistance to it has encountered fierce hostility in the past, and it will not be abandoned without a tremendous fight. The gold standard could go (glad to be rid of that!), Saigon abandoned, the Constitution itself slyly junked. But Darwinism will be defended to the bitter end.[12]

Creationism is, of course, unproven and unprovable, and thus cannot reasonably be considered a fact. Like Darwinism, it is clearly not subject to testing by the ordinary methods of experimental science. Therefore, it, too, does not, in a strict sense, qualify as a scientific theory. It is, therefore, only a postulate and may serve as a model within which attempts may be made to explain and correlate the evidence from the historical record (i.e., the fossil record) and to make predictions concerning the nature of future discoveries. But that is all it is.

Consequently, Darwinism and creationism are two peas in a pod, philosophically, scientifically, and theologically. Science, if it were truly neutral (or agnostic), would not permit one and exclude

---

[12] Bethell, *The American Spectator*, July 1994, page 17.

the other. It would either exclude them both, or include them both. Like me, many Americans are sick and tired of the double standard being inflicted on our culture. The deck has been stacked against supernaturalism for far too long and I, for one, don't intend to just sit around and take it anymore. The walls of pseudoscience that Darwinism had built around itself have started to come down, just like that wall between East and West Berlin did several years ago. And like communism, Darwinism is dead and I intend to do everything within my power to bury it.

Four decades ago, G.A. Kerkut, in his book, *Implication of Evolution*, wrote:

> ...*there is the theory that all living forms in the world have arisen from a single source which itself came from an inorganic form. This theory can be called the "General Theory of Evolution" and the evidence that supports it is not sufficiently strong to allow us to consider it as anything more than a working hypothesis.*[13]

There is, of course, a world of difference between a working hypothesis and an established fact. The "fact of evolution" (or macroevolution) is actually the faith of evolutionists in their particular world-view. No less a convinced evolutionist than Thomas H. Huxley admitted that:

> ... *"creation," in the ordinary sense of the word is perfectly conceivable. I find no difficulty in conceiving that, at some former period, this universe was not in existence, and that it made its appearance in six days (or instantaneously, if that is preferred), in consequence of the volition of some preexisting Being. Then, as now, the so-called a priori arguments against Theism and,*

---

[13] 1960, page 157.

given a Deity, against the possibility of creative acts, appeared to me to be devoid of reasonable foundation.[14]

If this is the conclusion of most evolutionists, then rhetorically I ask: Why not permit the origins debate in the science classrooms of America? What are they afraid of, the truth? How could permitting the teaching of the two models of origins, *neither* of which are truly worthy to be called scientific theories, be detrimental to modern science?

R. D. Alexander, Professor of Zoology at the University of Michigan, and an evolutionist, believes that:...

No teacher should be dismayed at efforts to present creation as an alternative to evolution in biology courses; indeed, at this moment creation is the only alternative to evolution. Not only is this worth mentioning, but a comparison of the two alternatives can be an excellent exercise in logic and reason. Our primary goal as educators should be to teach students to think, and such a comparison, particularly because it concerns an issue in which many have special interests or are even emotionally involved, may accomplish that purpose better than most others.[15]

Therefore, and finally, I conclude that the refusal of the establishment within scientific and educational circles to even consider creation as an alternative to evolution is based, above all, on the insistence upon a purely atheistic, materialistic, naturalistic, and mechanistic explanation of origins to the exclusion of an explanation based on theism or supernaturalism. Restricting the teaching

---

[14] T. H. Huxly, quoted in Life and Letters of Thomas Henry Huxley, vol. I, ed. L. Huxley, 1903, page 241.

[15] Anderson, in *Evolution versus Creationism: The Public Education Controversy*, ed. J. P. Zetterberg, 1983, page 91.

concerning origins to this one particular view constitutes indoctrination in a religious philosophy, specifically, philosophical (metaphysical) naturalism. This means that not only are acceptable rules of fairness being violated, but the Constitution's separation of church and state guarantees are being breached while the pursuit of true science is being shackled with dogma.

After years of interest in the creation/evolution controversy, I have concluded that the actual facts of science declare special creation to be the most reasonable explanation of origins. In my opinion, "In the beginning God created…" is still the most up-to-date statement that can be made about origins.

Christians who hitch their theological think-sos to the dogmas of Scientism, claiming, by doing so, to make the Bible more relevant to the modern (read "scientific") world are simply bowing to yet another of the sham gods of orthotalksy.

Chapter 12

Modern Churchanity, The God Of "Nice," And The "Age Of The Earth" Controversy

Look now at the behemoth, which I made along with you; he eats grass like an ox. See now, his strength is in his hips, and his power is in his stomach muscles. He moves his tail like a cedar; the sinews of his thighs are tightly knit. His bones are like beams of iron. He is the first of the ways of God; only He who made him can bring near His sword (Job 40:15-19).

Many view the Bible as a devotional prop of middle-class values. Modern Churchanity, with its various filters and interpretations, has succeeded, it thinks, in "taming" or "civilizing" the Bible. As a result, the Bible is thought to teach its adherents to be "nice" at all cost. "Niceness," then, has become the *sine qua non* of true religion for modern-day Christendom. But just as pacifists have misused Jesus' "turn the other cheek" statement to teach that one cannot engage in justice and righteousness (particularly in those cases where to do so would require the use of deadly force),[1] the prohibition against "offending a brother" is misunderstood and misapplied so as to uphold the middle-class idea that we must, above all, be "nice," even when such "niceness" is at the expense of truth. Consequently, and reflecting the wisdom that

---

[1] See Allan Turner, *The Christian & War*, 2006, pages 42-44.

comes from man, charging one's opponent with being mean-spirited has become an effective device for skirting arguments (or charges) being made by one's critics. Although such craftiness will continue to be rejected by men and women of integrity, it is a sad commentary on our times that so many have fallen prey to this carnal device.

In truth, the Bible is not middle-class, and it is certainly not "nice," as many today count "niceness." It is, instead (and has been so identified by various individuals and groups), a "dangerous," "uncivilized," "abrasive," "raw," "complicated," "aggressive," "scandalous," and "offensive" book. In fact, to its severest critics, the Bible is anything but "nice." If it were a movie being subjected to contemporary standards, its content would have to be "R-rated" in some places and "X-rated" in others.[2] That this can be said about the Bible will, no doubt, be offensive to some of you. After all, talking about the Bible this way isn't very "nice," is it? Even so, every honest and knowledgeable student of the Bible must admit that it covers the entire gamut of living. In addition to being the number one source for information about God, the Bible is also about men, women, sex, lies, truth, sin, goodness, fornication, adultery, murder, homosexuality, childbearing, virgins, whores, blasphemy, prayer, drunkenness, food, history, nature, ecology, poetry, politics, madness, rape, love, betrayal, salvation, damnation, temptation, angels, demons, and the like.

In addition, the Bible speaks of a spiritual world that few in our day and age can even understand, much less fully appreciate. But, and this is the point I'm trying to emphasize at this juncture, in

---

[2] Not that I think it is, mind you, but the statement stands on its own. This is particularly interesting when viewed in light of the recent brouhaha over the Motion Picture Association of America's labeling a movie "PG" because it had too much "Christian" religion.

conveying its spiritual truths, the Bible does not hesitate to accurately depict the real world in which we live. In telling its stories, it does not sanitize the lives of its characters, even its heroes. In other words, the Bible does not pull its punches, it does not beat around the bush, nor does it test the winds of change to learn what is politically correct, although all these reflect the wisdom of man. The Bible tells us how the world really is. Better yet, it tells us how we really are. Almost from the very beginning, the Bible begins to tell us of sin and all its terrible consequences. More importantly, it speaks of sin's most serious effect—the reality of being damned for eternity. But, praise God, it also speaks of the one and only remedy for this effect—the grace and mercy that comes in connection with the blood of Jesus Christ. However, for many, this is the Bible's most distasteful and offensive feature.

In a devastating assault on human pride and arrogance, the Bible's ego-shattering message is emphatically and unapologetically proclaimed in the name of a seemingly lowly and, perhaps, deranged Jew who died a despicable death almost two thousand years ago outside the walls of a city that rejected Him and His message. So how is it, these critics ask, that a tragically pathetic figure who could not even save Himself speak anything concerning the subject of salvation? In response to this, the apostle Paul, in his critique of man's wisdom in 1 Corinthians 1:22-25, wrote:

> *For Jews request a sign, and Greeks seek after wisdom; but we preach Christ crucified, to the Jews a stumbling block and to the Greeks foolishness, but to those who are called, both Jews and Greeks, Christ the power of God and the wisdom of God. Because the foolishness of God is wiser than men, and the weakness of God is stronger than men.*

Many today (and this could be abundantly documented) believe the apostle Paul was mean-spirited, uncivilized, narrow, and extremely bigoted for saying what He did about Jesus here and elsewhere in the Bible. Many of these think that what the apostle could have used was more polish concerning the social graces. Too bad poor ol' Paul didn't have access to Dale Carnegie's book, *How to Win Friends and Influence People.* And while we're on the subject, just how "nice" do you think it was of Jesus to offend the religiously pious of his day and throughout the intervening years by proclaiming: "I am the way, the truth, and the life. No one comes to the Father except through Me"?[3]

But what an audaciously haughty and offensive claim to be coming from one who, from the beginning, was thought by many to be His mother's illegitimate son (cf. John 8:41) and, in the end, it is claimed, could not even prevent His own crucifixion, even though He claimed to be God in the flesh. So, the Bible, with its exaltation of Jesus Christ as King of kings and Lord of lords, and its claim of containing true truth, isn't always "nice" by middle-class standards. Nevertheless, it remains the "power of God to salvation for everyone who believes" its message,[4] and we today, like all faithful students of the Word, must be careful that we are not ashamed of that message—a message, incidentally, that begins with Genesis 1:1.

The "Age Of The Earth" Controversy

Along these lines, and in view of the days of Creation row currently taking place among some New Testament Christians, I want to say that it makes me nervous when I hear some attempting to support their interpretation of the six days of Creation—an

---

[3] 1 John 14:6.
[4] Romans 1:16.

interpretation they claim encompasses billions of years—with the argument that such an interpretation will ultimately make the Bible less offensive to a more-educated, scientifically-oriented audience. I understand that this is not the only argument made for this position, nor is it even the main argument, but it is an argument nonetheless. As such, it appears to me to be a course that attempts a synthesis of God's so-called foolishness and man's alleged wisdom.

Some are on record as believing that the six days of Creation, when understood as consecutive days encompassing 144 hours, are more of an obstacle to genuine faith (particularly in a scientifically sophisticated audience) than is the claim of Jesus' resurrection. Frankly, and I've told some of these so, I find such an idea absolutely preposterous! Although these chafe (that's my interpretation) at my use of this word and adamantly defend their contention, their approach strikes me as being either terribly naive, which I seriously doubt, or a reflection of their unflagging allegiance to the idea that natural revelation is equal to special revelation, a view I think elevates natural revelation to the status of being the 67th book of the Bible.

Now, do I, like some, think all these brethren are heretics? No, I don't. Do I think they are all theistic evolutionists? No, I don't. In fact, because some have unfairly (perhaps ignorantly) accused them of these things, I feel like I've had to spend too much of my time defending these folks against these charges.

Brethren, if we hope to be effective in our criticism, we must have done our homework on this issue. In truth, all those who I know of who hold the position in question are adamantly opposed to theistic evolution and some have done some fine work in refuting it. The confusion occurs because of the required association of an ancient earth with the general theory of evolution. However, in these folks way of thinking, there is no correlation between these two things.

They think, and I believe they're right, that most Christians are guilty of swallowing the evolutionists' argument that their model demands a very old universe and earth, and have done so "hook, line and sinker!" They believe such claims to be nothing but evolutionist hubris. In other words, they are convinced one could grant evolutionists all the time they feel like they need for organic life to have evolved as it is today and it could still never happen—not even in a million trillion years.

I happen to agree with them. Therefore, the "age of the earth" issue is actually meaningless to the question of whether organic life somehow evolved from inorganic matter (and this in spite of the fact that the general theory of evolution cannot hope to remain viable without the billions of years it now claims for the age of the earth).

In fact, the Intelligent Design argument championed by Behe, Dembski and Johnson *et al.*, all of whom, incidentally, believe the earth is very old, has been quite effective in rattling the cage of mainline evolutionists, demonstrating the impossibility of the orthodox gradualism of the general theory of evolution.[5] So, when we argue with evolutionists about the error of their theory, we don't need to be afraid of granting them, for the sake of argument, all the time they feel they need, because even when we do so, they still don't have a shred of evidence that what they claim happened actually happened. In fact, those in question wholeheartedly affirm this—namely, that the evidence clearly favors Divine Creation, not evolutionism.

---

[5] The three men mentioned are Michael Behe, *Darwin's Black Box*, 1996, William A. Dembski, *Intelligent Design: The Bridge Between Science & Theology*, 1999, and Phillip E. Johnson, *Darwin On Trial*, 1993. There are others, of course, but these men were in the vanguard of the Intelligent Design movement.

So, Then, What's The Problem?

Having said all this (and I believe fairness demands it), the question still remains: Do I think those in question are wrong about the age of the earth? Yes, I do. However, and this has disappointed some of my own critics, I decided many years ago not to make the age of the earth, *per se*, a test of fellowship. In my own mind, I do not believe that Christians who think the earth is billions of years old are necessarily lost.

As a young Christian, I believed theistic evolution to be the most viable answer to the seeming conflict between science and the Bible. I was wrong. But even as I look back on my immature thinking, I do not believe that position, in and of itself, placed my soul in jeopardy. I continued to believe that the Bible was God's divine revelation to man. I still believed in God and was thankful for the remission of sins He offered me in connection with His Son's blood. Again, you may disagree with me about this, but I do not believe my theistic evolution position automatically damned me to hell.

Because I take this particular position, some think I believe the whole age of the earth thing is irrelevant, or as some might say, a "tempest in a teapot." But you'd be wrong to think so. In fact, I reserve some of my strongest criticisms for those who seem to all too flippantly dismiss this debate as "much to do about nothing." The subject is not irrelevant and goes to the very heart of who we are as a people. I have expressed these concerns in some detail, and in various venues, not just to those in question, but to others as well.

Furthermore, and here's some advice for young-earth creation (YEC) apologists, anyone who approaches the age of the earth question thinking that old-earth creationists (OECs) are intellectual slouches when it comes to either science or the Bible is in for a rude awakening. If you're going to spar with these folks you had better make sure you've got on full body armor. Some of these folks are powerful in their OEC apologetic and it is clear that they are serious about their study of the Bible, as well. No, these individuals are no dawdlers, and anyone who faces them thinking they are will more than likely walk away a bit bruised and bloodied, metaphorically speaking.

A Readiness, It Seems, To "Explain Away" Scripture

However, OECs, in their efforts to defend their position, make interpretations that are highly unlikely when viewed solely from a scriptural standpoint. In addition, they are not able to confine their hermeneutic to Genesis 1. Instead, they use it as the interpreter of a wide variety of Bible subjects. *It is just here that I am most troubled.* Why? Because it is what OECs are willing to do with, and say about, God's Word that is most disturbing to me. Their approach reminds me of the theological wrangling about words that is so common among liberal theologians today—a system that was resoundingly condemned in God's Word a long time ago (cf. 2 Timothy 2:14).

Although I do not believe anyone is obligated to exercise faith in "flood geology" as articulated by John C. Whitcomb and Henry M. Morris *et al.*,[6] OECs frequently entertain the idea that the Genesis Flood was a localized affair; and if not a localized affair, then at least an event that, although universal, was extremely tranquil and caused little, if any, changes on the earth. And why is this? Because large scale catastrophism, which seems to be a reasonable extrapolation of the effects of a truly global flood, throws a monkey

---

[6] Their book, *The Genesis Flood*, 1961, still holds some of the best arguments for Flood geology.

wrench into the assumptions of OECs who are, if I might be permitted to use the term, capital "U" uniformitarianists.

Capital "U" Uniformitarianists

What do I mean by capital "U" uniformitarianists? Specifically this: Capital "U" uniformitarianists believe that current natural laws and processes are sufficient to explain the origin and development of all things. Capital "U" uniformitarianists, without hesitation, apply their assumptions all the way back to the "Big Bang" that is alleged to have occurred at the beginning of the universe. Consequently, the great cataclysmic events that reasonable men and women have inferred from the Genesis Flood—events that would have dramatically affected the earth's surface—are systematically rejected. Accepting, as they do, the supposed geologic column,[7] OECs extol what they think is the overwhelming evidence for a very old universe (some 14-plus billion years) and earth (approximately 4.5 billion years). Thinking that their interpretation of the scientific data is the testimony of "natural revelation," they freely apply this interpretation to the Bible. Therefore, to their way of thinking, the six days of creation must be expanded to represent billions of years.

Elevating "Science" To "The 67th Book" Of The Bible

Furthermore, because their alleged geologic clock separates the extinction of dinosaurs and the appearance of man by some 60 to

---

[7] The supposed geologic column is the one you see represented in school textbooks that purports to show the uniform nature of the geologic strata as it exists in the world. Of course, its base is uniformitarianism, which simply assumes the thing to be proved.

70 million years, OECs believe that dinosaurs and man did not coexist. In coming to this conclusion, OECs have raised their interpretation of the scientific data to the status of the 67th book of the Bible. They don't like it when YECs say this, but this is exactly what they have done. In fact, some have made it clear in their writings that they believe natural revelation (which must be interpreted) and special revelation (which also must be interpreted) are *equally* God's revelation and, because this is the case, each can be used to interpret the other. However, and here's the dig, when special revelation appears to contradict natural revelation, OECs clearly give natural revelation precedence. After all, as they repeatedly point out, they are dealing with "real physical evidence," that is, things you can "really see." Consequently, they clearly make one means of revelation more "equal" than the other.

Of course, the Bible tells us that the Christian is to walk by faith, not by sight,[8] and this is what bothers me and many others about the OEC position. Yes, God has made Himself known through natural revelation, but for many Christians, God's special revelation always takes precedence over man's understanding of natural revelation. But, when the OEC hermeneutic is coupled with the fact that there is no unquestioned evidence of dinosaur and human fossils occupying the same strata, OECs become convinced that YECs err when arguing that dinosaurs and man were contemporary. "Where is the evidence for such thinking?," they challenge. When one retorts, "What do you mean by 'Where is the evidence?,'" they reply, "Where are the written records of mankind that refer to dinosaurs and humans coexisting?" When one answers, "In the Bible!," one should get ready to be subjected to a rather perturbed expression of incredulity.

---

[8] See 2 Corinthians 5:7.

How This Kind Of Interpretation Works

In fact, OECs have become so convinced that dinosaurs went extinct many millions of years before man was created, they have started to claim that behemoth—mentioned in Job 40:15-24, and which the Creator called "chief of the ways of God" (suggesting that it may have been the largest land animal God made)—"can't be a dinosaur." To add to this, and once again appealing to the geologic column, it is claimed that because no dinosaur fossils have ever been found in the bronze age, which they believe coincides with the age of the patriarchs, dinosaurs and man simply did not coexist. But, according to the most natural reading of Genesis 1, the creation of dinosaurs (whether they were sea or land creatures) was separated from the creation of man by, at the most, a 48-hour period that would have encompassed the whole of day five and six.

Apart from the assumptions made in connection with the geologic column, there is no reason to believe that dinosaurs became extinct some 60-70 million years before man came into being. And it seems very unlikely that modern man, inundated with depictions of what dinosaurs would have looked like, could read the description of behemoth in Job 40:15-24 and not think a very large dinosaur (like a Brachiosaurus) was being described. Now, can I say conclusively that behemoth was a dinosaur? No, I can't. But I can say that a dinosaur is the first thing that pops into my mind when I read these verses and, for the life of me, I can't think of anything else it could be.

The effort to which some OECs have gone to avoid the obvious borders on the ludicrous. For example, one went into a rather elaborate description of behemoth as a hippopotamus. When he got to the tail, which the Scriptures describe as being like a "cedar," he talked about the rather short tail of the hippopotamus being stubby and stiff, characteristics which he claimed, granting the writer of Job "poetic license," could conceivably be described as a "tail like a cedar." But not unless we're talking about one of those little bonsai cedars for which the Japanese are famous. Such shenanigans are, at best, simply ludicrous and, at worst, totally reprehensible. The fact that this brother is otherwise a very good Bible student is an illustration of just how far some will go in their use of a uniformitarian understanding of natural revelation as a means for "interpreting" the sixty-six books of the Bible.

Consequently, I am more than a bit put off by a Christian who arrogantly claims that behemoth "can't be" a dinosaur. The only reason for anyone to do so is for the reasons mentioned above, and this means that one is guilty of reading into the Scriptures his own preconceived ideas. Now, am I being mean-spirited for saying this? I don't think so. Unfortunately, those who have imbibed the sentiments of the age will probably think so. In fact, and as I previously pointed out, the charge of being mean-spirited is all one needs to start hollering in order to protect himself from having to answer for what he is doing to the Bible with his natural-revelation-is-the-67th-book-of-the-Bible hermeneutic.

As I know many of these OEC brethren to be very good Bible students, and as I know firsthand of the spiritually conservative backgrounds of which they have been a part, it seems strange to me that they would not have anticipated, and therefore understood, the strong opposition they have received from a great many of their fellow Christians. But to oppose OECism, even when one does so frankly, openly, and forcefully, is not necessarily mean-spirited, although this could and, in my opinion, does describe the actions of a few YECs. But there are OECs who are just as guilty. However, I am not really interested in the wranglings of brethren on both sides of this issue who are yet carnal in their thinking and actions. What I'm interested in, and it seems to me like it is getting harder and harder to do this today, is dealing with the issues/differences that stand between the OEC and YEC positions. These differences are not irrelevant, and even those OECs who appear to give the impression they are, make it clear they think we YECs ought to "repent" because our position "sets up young people for a loss of faith." Such certainly doesn't sound like OECs think this issue to be irrelevant, does it? But, it gets worse.

Death: "Science" Vs. The Bible

Because OECs believe dinosaurs died out sixty-seventy million years before man, they believe death pre-existed Adam's sin. Consequently, they believe the death of animals was an integral part of God's "very good" creation way before man ever came onto the scene. But is this what the Bible teaches? No, it isn't. The Bible, in 1 Corinthians 15:21, makes it clear that "death came by man." So, do animals suffer death because it is a natural part of God's "very good" creation, or do they suffer death as a result of Adam's sin? Genesis 3:14 makes it clear that "the serpent" was "cursed more than all cattle, and more than every beast of the field." This means that animals, along with man, were cursed as a result of Adam's sin.

When one factors into this the biblical idea that *nephesh* creatures[9] are distinct from plants, which do not have *being* and are not, therefore, nephesh, then one understands how the eating of plants, which animals and humans were permitted by God to do—and this before sin entered into the world[10]—did not involve

---

[9] The term means "living" and refers to animals or "living creatures" (cf. Genesis 1:24,30) and human beings or "living souls" (cf. Genesis 2:7).

[10] See Genesis 1:29-30.

"death," or the loss of *nephesh* existence. Physical death, then, as the Bible says, "came by man."

Furthermore, the fossil record, along with telling the story of the death of *nephesh* creatures, also tells the story of thorns and thistles, which were a part of the cursing of the ground for Adam's sake. In contrast, OECs envision a garden of Eden sitting on top of a fossil record (including thorns and thistles) millions of years old. If this were true, then the "bondage of corruption" to which the *whole creation* was subjected took place before Adam's sin. However, that physical death itself was a consequence of the "curse" that came upon the "whole creation" as the result of Adam's sin is hard to miss when one carefully studies the Bible and does not try to explain away the teaching of verses like Romans 8:20-22, which say:

> *For the creation was subjected to futility, not willingly, but because of Him who subjected it in hope; because the creation itself also will be delivered from the bondage of corruption into the glorious liberty of the children of God. For we know that the whole creation groans and labors with birth pangs together until now.*

When one factors in the next verse, where Paul makes a distinction between himself, as a human being, and the rest of creation, then it is clear that he is speaking of that "new heaven and...new earth in which righteousness dwells,"[11] that is, paradise restored,[12] as compared to paradise lost.[13]

---

[11] 2 Peter 3:13.
[12] See Revelation 22:14.
[13] See Genesis 3:23.

So, if the whole creation has been subjected to "futility" and the "bondage of corruption" or "decay" as the result of one man's sin, then death and dying were not a part of God's original "very good" creation. But, in order to justify imposing a particular interpretation of "natural revelation" onto the Bible, some are willing to wreak theological havoc on more than just Genesis One and the Days of Creation. Consequently, it remains my firm belief that the think-sos of men, whether theological, philosophical, or scientific, must ultimately bow to the objective standard of God's Word. In other words, "If anyone speaks, let him speak as the oracles of God."[14]

The Bible is God's special revelation to man. As such, it is far superior to the natural revelation He has made of Himself in His creation, a creation that has been sadly marred by sin. This is not said to denigrate natural revelation, for God has said that because of it man is without excuse for not believing that He is. This is, instead, a reminder that natural revelation, even when it has been properly interpreted, was never intended to supersede the Bible, and I think that anyone who thinks it does is headed down a path I don't intend to travel.

OECs, trying to argue against what it appears Romans 8:20-22 is clearly teaching, make fun of "the whole creation" groaning, including "fruit flies," along with "bugs and slugs." But in doing so I want you to take notice that they don't spend any time exegeting the passage itself. I have asked them to do this, but I'm still waiting for them to do so. Instead, we get speechifying on what it can't be. Why? Because of the fossil record with all its evidence of suffering and dying, and their uniformitarian interpretation of it, that's why! So, if this isn't a nature-as-the-67th-book-of-the-Bible

---

[14] 1 Peter 4:11a.

hermeneutic, or nature as yet "another passage" for interpreting Scripture, then what would you call it?

"Niceness" Vs. The Truth

In concluding my remarks here, let me say this about the dialogues that take place between YECs and OECs: there are dialogues and then there are dialogues. Some dialogues are exercises in "niceness," simply pretending that our disagreements make little or no difference. To such dialogues, OECs and YECs or, for that matter, almost anyone else can be invited without difficulty. We can all exchange "warm fuzzies" and feel good about having made the effort, as this serves to demonstrate how "reasonable" and "nice" we believe ourselves to be.

On the other hand, there is dialogue in service to the truth. Unfortunately, the practitioners of Modern Churchanity and "niceness," a group that shies away from the objective standard of God's word, have decided that the philosophies and traditions of men, when coupled with the "basic principles of the world," are just fine and dandy.[15] Consequently, they believe the essence of their religion is to be "nice" to everyone so we can "all just get along," as the infamous Rodney King blurted out in supposed frustration.

Unfortunately, these modern-day practitioners of Churchanity do not seem the least bit interested in dialogue of any kind. Monologue has become their preferred *modus operandi*. Critics, who are usually deemed by these folks to be raining on their "be happy" parade, are subjected to tired clichés, cheap irony, and sophomoric rhetorical tricks. Nevertheless, when they do so, they invoke a now predictable tone that, not so nicely (how ironic is this?),

---

[15] cf. Colossians 2:8.

attempts to neatly pigeonhole all who disagree with them as being just a bunch of mean-spirited cranks who are always getting up on the wrong side of the bed. Undoubtedly, the devil loves such irony.

"Keep Yourselves From Idols"[16]

Idolatry, the kind we moderns are so susceptible to, does not have to be a physical construct sitting on a material altar somewhere. Instead, it can be an idea, a way of thinking, that causes us to forget our prior allegiance is to God and His word. I close, then, with the words of the apostle Paul who said, in 1 Corinthians 1:20-29:

> *Where is the wise? Where is the scribe? Where is the disputer of this age? Has not God made foolish the wisdom of this world? For since, in the wisdom of God, the world through wisdom did not know God, it pleased God through the foolishness of the message preached to save those who believe.... For you see your calling, brethren, that not many wise according to the flesh, not many mighty, not many noble, are called. But God has chosen the foolish things of the world to put to shame the wise, and God has chosen the weak things of the world to put to shame the things which are mighty; and the base things of the world and the things which are despised God has chosen, and the things which are not, to bring to nothing the things that are, that no flesh should glory in His presence.*

---

[16] 1 John 5:21.

Chapter 13

The "Only In And Through The Word" Bunch

Having a form of godliness but denying its power. And from such people turn away! (2 Timothy 3:5).

Alexander Campbell's favorite philosopher was John Locke (1632-1704). He is one of mine, as well. But I am afraid that Locke's rationalistic approach unduly influenced Campbell. Consequently, Campbell rationalized the working of the Holy Spirit in conversion and limited His influence to the written Word. It was his belief that "if the Spirit of God has spoken all its arguments" in the Bible, then "all the power of the Holy Spirit which can operate on the human mind is spent."[1] It is not surprising, then, that Campbell's close friend and biographer, Dr. Robert Richardson, who preached Campbell's funeral, wrote the following in a letter to Isaac Errett:

The philosophy of John Locke with which Bro. Campbell's mind was deeply imbued in youth has insidiously mingled itself with almost all great points in the reformation and has been all the whole like an iceberg in the way—chilling the heart and

---

[1] See the Campbell-Rice Debate, Henry Clay presiding, Lexington, Kentucky, 1843. This was Mr. Campbell's last public debate.

benumbing the hands, and impeding all progress in the right direction.[2]

Although I am not convinced that Richardson, rather than Campbell, had a better grip on the "right way," I do believe Richardson was right in rejecting the "Word alone" vs. the "Spirit alone" dichotomy that had arisen in the Restoration Movement. But before anyone thinks me an enemy of Campbell (and some have), please understand that I hold him and much of his work in high esteem. And although I think Campbell was right in trying to counter the "better felt than told experience" of the Calvinists, who taught that one was saved by the direct operation of the Holy Spirit apart from the Word of God, his conclusion was, in my opinion, quite incorrect. The Holy Spirit certainly works through the Word in conversion. In fact, no one can be converted apart from the Word. But, and this is very important, the Bible nowhere teaches that the Holy Spirit is limited to working "only in and through the Word." Unfortunately, this is a mistake that many among us have continued to make. Some have even taken the next step and are teaching that "God [viz., the totality of Who and What He is] works only in and through the Word today."

An Example

While discussing the continued activity of demons today with a fellow preacher (and I'm not talking about demon possession), I pointed out that the Bible says we are engaged in a battle "against

---

[2] Goodnight's transcript of Richardson's private papers; a letter from Bethphage, July 16, 1857. Also Cloyd Goodnight and Dwight E. Stevenson, *Home to Bethphage: A Biography of Robert Richardson*, 1949, page 122.

principalities, against powers, against the rulers of the darkness of this age, against spiritual hosts of wickedness in heavenly places."[3] Furthermore, I pointed out it had been prophesied that some would give heed to deceiving spirits and doctrines of demons.[4] In connection with this, I mentioned that the Bible teaches there is a wisdom that is derived from demons,[5] and that the battle we are engaged in seems to be centered on the mind.[6] It was my point that these passages clearly teach us that the Devil can fill our hearts, blind and corrupt our minds and, by the use of deception, take us captive to do his will. But, according to this preacher, such was true only during the miraculous age. Satan and his agents, according to this preacher, can no longer do these things today. When asked why, he replied, in part, that God worked only in and through the Word today and, therefore, if Satan and his agents were allowed to influence our minds, then they would be more powerful today than God.

This is exactly the kind of thinking I am trying to pinpoint. Where does the Bible teach, either through direct statement, approved example, or necessary inference, that God works only in and through the Word today? Where is the teaching that says God cannot influence our minds apart from the Word? Of course, one may counter by asking, "Where is the passage that says God does influence the mind independent of the Word?" This is a good question. In answering it, I call your attention to James 1:5. In this passage, we are taught that God gives wisdom to His children when they ask for it. Notice that this wisdom comes as a direct result of

---

[3] Ephesians 6:12.
[4] See 1 Timothy 4:1.
[5] See James 3:14-17.
[6] See Acts 5:3; 2 Corinthians 4:4; 11:3; 2 Timothy 2:26.

prayer, not study—although I believe it is safe to conclude this happens in a way not totally divorced from the serious study of God's Word. Therefore, the Bible teaches that God can, and does, somehow influence the mind apart from the Word—and by this I mean the Word as the agent. If this were the only passage we were able to cite, and it's not, it would prove, quite conclusively, that God is not limited to working only in and through the Word today.

Modern Sadducees

I am afraid that many, "not knowing the Scriptures nor the power of God," have become nothing much more than modern-day Sadducees.[7] Like the Deists, these seem to worship a God who no longer actively works in His creation. Their secularized gospel, although it sometimes gives lip-service to God's providence, says that when good things happen, they happen because of chance, accident, planning, or work. In such matters, God's providence is not really taken into consideration—after all, "God works only in and through the Word today," they tell us. Likewise, when bad things happen, they happen for the same reasons. Satan's activities are simply not factored in—after all, if Satan were directly involved, then he would have more power than God. Why? "Because God," they remind us, "works only in and through the Word today." Such teaching may seem orthodox to more than a few Christians, but I am convinced it has its roots in Locke's 17th century rationalism. The following examples come from Wayne Wells, a gospel preacher, concerning exchanges and conversations he engaged in with several gospel preachers:

---

[7] See Matthew 22:29.

In an email exchange, one preacher from a western state claimed the only thing Christians can ask from God is the forgiveness of sins. He said we can thank God for what He already created but cannot ask Him to do anything else or that would be a miracle. He wrote, "No, I do not believe in any kind of material or spiritual providence by God, Christ nor the Holy Spirit in this day and age."[8]

He went on to say:

In a conversation, several preachers from a northern state claimed the only way God can influence nations is by His Word. They said the citizens will either obey or reject the Scriptures. If they obey, they will be honest and hard working so the nation will prosper. If they reject the Scriptures, they will be lazy and dishonest and cause the nation to crumble, and this is the only influence God has over the nations today![9]

He rightly concluded that section of his article with:

Such Biblical ignorance and perversions are breathtaking in their implications. How did a people become so ignorant of the hand of the Lord? God asked Israel, "Is My hand shortened at all that it cannot redeem? Or have I no power to deliver?" (Isaiah 50:2). They had no faith that God worked in their lives. The lack of understanding today proves again there is no new thing under the sun.

It is most unfortunate that many Christians living at the beginning of the 21st century are more comfortable with naturalistic

---

[8] Wayne Wells, "Campbellism vs. Prayer," *re:thinking magazine*, April 2006, at www.allanturner.com/magazine/Wells009.html.
[9] *Ibid.*

rationalism than they are with the supernaturalism taught in the Bible. This ought not to be.

God's Providence

If we are going to teach that God's providence is real, and that prayer is, in fact, effectual, then we must not teach that God works only in and through the Word today. As Sovereign of the Universe, God exercises control over nature, nations, and individuals. Currently, Jesus Christ rules as "Lord of lords." The Bible says He has all authority in heaven and on earth[10] and "upholds all things by the word of His power."[11] Are we to think that He does this only in and through the written Word? Surely we can see how such thinking would dethrone the Lord in the minds of such folks. Moreover, the very fact that we exist proves that God is actively at work in His creation, for "in Him [viz., Jesus] all things consist" or hold together.[12] Without Jesus' continuing work, everything would simply disintegrate.

Furthermore, in addition to *general* providence, there is the *special* providence promised to the church. Paul tells us that "all things work together for good to those who love God,"[13] and that He provides us with all our needs.[14] He tells us that we always have "sufficiency in all things."[15] In Matthew 6:23-33, the Lord Himself says that those who will put the kingdom of God first in their lives

---

[10] See John 17:2.
[11] Hebrews 1:3.
[12] See Colossians 1:17.
[13] Romans 8:28.
[14] See Philippians 4:19.
[15] 2 Corinthians 9:8-11.

will have all their physical needs taken care of. Are we to think that this will happen only in and through the Word?

Indeed, the Bible teaches that Christians ought to study and pray. But, if God today works only in and through the Word, then we ought, in all honesty, to quit praying and use this time for more Bible study. If not, why not? In truth, Restoration slogans and ideas, even when they come from the esteemed Alexander Campbell, are useful only as long as they reflect the truths taught in God's Word.

But How About Miracles?

Some believe, and I think quite erroneously, that in order for God to be actively at work in His creation today, He would have to be performing miracles. This view seems to ignore the fact that most of God's activities in both the Old and New Testaments were non-miraculous. The story of Joseph is but one of the many examples of this. Although men, with all their lusts, jealousies, and deceptions, were exercising their free wills in the matter of Joseph, he could say, "you meant evil against me; but God meant it for good, in order to bring it about as it is this day, to save many people alive."[16] Further, the Bible attributes David's success against the lion, bear, and Goliath to the help of God.[17] Are we to label these "miraculous"? The Scriptures teach that the Lord was able to work a great victory through Shammah when he stood in his own bean field.[18] Where was the miracle? Consequently, when we stand in our own bean fields today, can't God work victories through us

---

[16] Genesis 50:20; 45:5-8.
[17] See 1 Samuel 17:37, 45-47.
[18] See 2 Samuel 23:11-12.

The Christian & Idolatry

without performing miracles? And when He does so, is it correct for His followers to claim He is working only in and through the Word?

The Bible tells us that God can deliver us from the evil one,[19] and that He can open doors of opportunity for us.[20] Can He? Does He? By faith, we can say, "Yes!" Does God need to perform a miracle to do so? Most certainly not! Therefore, those who believe and trust in the Lord can confidently sing, "Lord I believe, yes, I believe, I cannot doubt or be deceived; the eye that sees each sparrow fall, His unseen hand is in it all."

In contemplating the majesty of Jehovah, Jack Cottrell, in his excellent book, *What The Bible Says About God The Ruler*, wrote:

> *Who is this God who holds the entire universe in the palm of his hand, and preserves it from oblivion by the mere force of his will? Who is this One whose power and presence penetrate and envelope every particle of the cosmos? What kind of God holds the reins of nature so that clouds turn, snow falls, thunder roars, and stars explode at his command? What kind of God knows every star and sparrow by name, and cares about them? What kind of God is this who can endow the crown of his creation with free will and still maintain constant control over the events and flow of history? How shall we describe the God who turns kings' hearts wherever he wills; who metes out life and death, blessing and calamity, whose power bursts forth in signs and wonders in the heavens and on the earth?*[21]

---

[19] See Matthew 6:13; 2 Thessalonians 3:3.
[20] See 1 Corinthians 16:7; Colossians 4:2-3; Revelation 3:8.
[21] 1984, page 265.

How thankful we ought to be that this one true God is our God. We must not think, say, or do anything that would take away from His glory and majesty. Limiting Him to working only in and through the written Word does just that, and is, I am convinced, a serious mistake.

Therefore, let us not be guilty of limiting the Lord of the universe to working only in and through the Word today, thereby making Him just another of the sham gods of orthotalksy.

Chapter 14

Modern-Day Shibboleths

If a man speak, let him speak as the oracles of God (1 Peter 4:11).

In Judges 12:6, the Hebrew word transliterated as "shibboleth" was used to expose an Ephraimite who was trying to hide his identity from the Jews. He was evidently unable to pronounce the word the way a Jew would, and he paid for it with his life. Today, *shibboleth* has come to be identified as a word or phrase that marks a particular group or cause; a catchword or slogan, if you will. In this chapter, I want to address the use of modern-day shibboleths among New Testament Christians. But to do so, it will be helpful for us to go back over some previously plowed ground.

As demonstrated ealier, it is impossible to make distinctions between God, His essence, and His attributes.[1] If Jehovah ceased to be anything less than what He is, He could not be the God who has identified Himself in the Scriptures. Consequently, it is never correct to think of God apart from His essence or attributes. What this means is that God does not have an essence, He *is* His essence, and He does not have attri- butes, He *is* His attributes.

But there are some who argue that the attributes of God can be stripped from Him. In other words, they argue that God's attributes can be separated from His essence, either in part or wholly. One such Christian had this to say:

---

[1] See Chapters 2 and 8, specifically.

This difference in the essence of God and the attributes of God has been noted, not just by denominational writers, but by some brethren as well. Brother Roy H. Lanier, Sr. wrote, "While the attributes of God are 'distinguishing characteristics of the divine nature,' we must be careful to view them as something apart from the essence of that divine nature. To view the sum of the attributes as God is to deny the personality of God." But unfortunately we have some brethren doing exactly that. One has written, "God is His characteristics and attributes."[2]

Although this un-named brother gives no citation for the Lanier statement, it is taken from page 24 of Lanier's book on God entitled, *The Timeless Trinity*. I have read this book and found it quite useful. However, I have not always agreed with all of Lanier's conclusions and, in this instance, I find myself disagreeing with him. Ontologically (i.e., by reason of His Being), the "I AM THAT I AM"[3] cannot be anything other than what He *is*, and He *is*, as has already been shown from Scripture, self-existent, eternal, infinite and immutable.

It is important to note that bro. Lanier believed Jesus to be the "divine-human" or "God-man" who, while here on earth, "retained all the attributes of Deity."[4] On page 242, he wrote that Jesus "could not cease to possess the essential attributes of God, for he is immutable." So, unlike the one who quoted him, Lanier did not believe that the "divine nature" could ever be divested of the "attributes of Deity."

Now, when the one who quoted Lanier wrote: *"But unfortunately we have some brethren doing exactly that. One has written,*

---

[2] Citation not given to protect the guilty.
[3] Exodus 3:14.
[4] *The Timeless Trinity*, p. 268.

'God is His characteristics and attributes,'" he could have been, and probably was, quoting me, for I have made it clear in my preaching, teaching, and writing that I believe God *is* His attributes and characteristics. Therefore, I happily plead guilty, whether I'm the one being referred to or not. However, and I need to emphasize this here once more, what I have *not* said about this subject is as important as what I have said.

I have not said, for example, and I do not believe, that any particular attribute of God is God. For example, and this, too, was noted in a previous chapter, I am not saying that any particular attribute of God is God. In other words, I have never said that "Love," for instance, "is God." What I believe and teach is what the Bible says in 1 John 4:8 and 16, namely, that "God is love." Why is it, then, that we have come to the point where one who believes and teaches what the Bible says on this subject can be criticized for believing and teaching exactly what the Bible says on this subject? And, more importantly, why do more than a few Christians believe that such criticism is actually valid?

The answer, I think, should be obvious: *It is clear that some among us no longer believe what the Bible teaches.* These have made fun of the "God-man" doctrine of incarnation. They scoff and call "silly" the idea that Jesus could have been "100% deity and 100% human." They teach that the *Logos*, upon coming to earth, divested Himself of His "divinity" and "godhood," and became "a man, just a man," "an ordinary man just like you and me." Some of these argue that Jesus, like every other man, actually "lusted" while here on this earth and, like every other man, faced death fearing that there may not really be a God or life beyond the grave.

When these ideas first surfaced, I thought them to be indicative of a shocking, but small, digression among conservative, non-institutional churches of Christ. I thought the reaction to a doctrine so clearly unbiblical would be so immediate and overwhelmingly unfavorable that, once it was openly exposed, those who held such a position would be forced either to repent or, else, suffer the deserved consequences of being publicly identified as those who taught error. I was wrong.

Unfortunately, the non-existent or, when it did come, slow, seemingly reluctant reaction of many to these ideas has, in my opinion, emboldened these folks to obscure their error by exploiting the false idea that the whole controversy was never more than a "preacher squabble" which was, in turn, aggravated by the esoteric character of semantics and the alleged mean-spirited, nasty, and supposedly cantankerous nature of certain personalities. But such charges were an obvious smoke screen, or at least it seems so to me, and the Bible teaches us to expect nothing less from those who teach things that are not true.[5]

Actually, the false ideas these folks preach and teach were accurately identified from the very beginning of this controversy. They were not being misrepresented or misquoted, as they claimed. Their words were not taken out of context, as their defenders allege. In fact, it is the very context of their writing and preaching that was used to expose them. That evidence has been presented in various forums and it is plain, clear, and incontrovertible. Nevertheless, influenced by the bombast, ridicule, and *ad hominem* diatribes of those who teach such things, the "jury," in some places, was slow to return its verdict.

In the meantime, the doctrine of these preachers/teachers continues to be defended by "faithful" brethren.[6] Others, who would not themselves take the false position being advocated, malign and

---

[5] See Colossians 2:8; 1 Timothy 6:20; Ephesians 4:14; 2 Corinthians 2:11; 2 Timothy 3:1-9; 2 Peter 2:1-22, *et cetera*.

[6] As far as I know, this may continue to be the case, although many have tried to publicly distance themselves from such ideas.

wag their tongues at those who have exposed the error. Others, still, sit on the sidelines, hoping the whole thing will blow over without anybody ever really noticing. These were heard to say, "The last thing we need is another controversy," or "If we can't invoke Romans 14 in our differences, then we [the 'we' meaning conservative, non-institutional churches of Christ—AT] are going to divide and splinter into a thousand different groups."

These last two groups, at least in part, ware made up of those who worship at the various totems of Self. These had learned to accentuate the positive while avoiding the negative at all cost, and had no love for "Mister In-Between." Instead of contending "earnestly for the faith which was once and for all delivered to the saints,"[7] which takes moral courage, these were much more comfortable with the "feel good about yourself" gospel of Self-Love—a gospel that has continued to excite the minds and tickle the ears of a lost and dying world and a faithless church. Yes, these folks continued to utter the shibboleths of a bygone era, but, in truth, they no longer had the stomachs for fighting the good fight of faith.

A prime example of this attitude is to be found in the following article which was taken from a church bulletin and was entitled, "Why We Aren't Growing":

> <u>*Desire For a Fight*</u>. *One of the main reasons we have seen a decline in conversions is that we are constantly looking for fights among ourselves. No sooner has one "issue" been defeated (with no small losses) than we are busy looking around for the next big "issue." From institutionalism to Grace-Fellowship—Calvinism to Deity-Humanity of Christ we eagerly wade [up to] our necks in the blood of sometimes innocent Christians (i.e. babes in*

---

[7] Jude 3.

Christ). This is not to say that the truth should not be defended, but I think a party spirit prevails among God's people at this time.

Notice the shibboleth: *"This is not to say that the truth should not be defended."* But on the other hand, if one decides to defend the truth on any of the issues mentioned, he is already branded a spiritual gunslinger with an itchy trigger finger.

Brethren, as the things critiqued in the chapters of this book demonstrate, we are drifting and do not seem to realize just how far we are from shore. To defend the truth, one must be willing to *stand against* falsehood. Therefore, we must not give lip-service to defending the truth and then cowardly shoot in the back those who believe and act upon what we say. This would, after all, be unconscionable.

In truth, the "Jesus divested Himself of His Deity and became a man, just an ordinary man like you and me" bunch were/are extolling a Jesus who was/is just another of the sham gods of orthotalksy.

But whether the issue actually being contested at any given moment is the deity of Jesus or the multitude of other important issues that confront us today, Christians who will be true to the Lordship of Jesus Christ cannot just engage in shibboleths, that is, just "talking the talk," as it is said, but they must be willing to "walk the walk," as well.[8]

---

[8] See 1 Peter 4:11.

Chapter 15

Our Theological Chickens Are Coming Home To Roost

But there were also false prophets among the people, even as there will be false teachers among you, who will secretly bring in destructive heresies, even denying the Lord who bought them, and bring on themselves swift destruction. And many will follow their destructive ways, because of whom the way of truth will be blasphemed (2 Peter 2:1-2).

According to Ecclesiastes 12:13, the whole duty of man is to fear the Creator of the universe and keep His commandments. This is not something just for those who are in covenant relationship with God through Christ, but for all mankind. The Creator has natural dominion over us even before He has authority over us by consent when we are converted. Why? Because, quite frankly, He is the Creator/Sovereign of the universe—He's the Creator and we are the creatures; He's the Potter and we are the clay!

Consequently, He has the authority to make demands upon us and we are under obligation to obey His commands. Apart from this understanding there are no real ethical norms (i.e., *What should I do?*) or obligations (i.e., *Why should I do it?*); no such things as absolute norms of conduct—no such things as moral absolutes. This, we learn in Romans 1:18-32, is why those who wanted to satisfy their own lusts chose not to retain in their minds the proper concept of God as Creator/Sovereign. They did not "glorify" God, nor were they "thankful," therefore, they "exchanged the truth of God for a lie, and worshipped and served the creature rather than the Creator."

True religion (i.e., man made in the image of God, cf. Genesis 1:26-27) and false religion (i.e., God created in the image of man, cf. Romans 1:22-23) are complete opposites. The antagonism between these two is constant. Consequently, the apostle Paul warned, "Beware lest anyone cheat you through philosophy and empty deceit, according to the tradition of men, according to the basic principles of the world, and not according to Christ."[1] In this passage we can clearly see the antagonism between the "tradition of men" and "basic principles of this world" and the teaching of Christ. As Jesus said elsewhere, there are only two sources for religion—God or man.[2]

In 2 Corinthians 10:4-5, Paul wrote: "For the weapons of our warfare are not carnal but mighty in God for pulling down strongholds, casting down arguments and every high thing that exalts itself against the knowledge of God, bringing every thought into captivity to the obedience of Christ." Making use of military metaphors, the apostle is contrasting vain philosophy (viz., man-made religion) with the truth revealed in the Bible (viz., God-breathed or inspired religion). He is contrasting the secular world view with the Biblical world view.

Our weapons, he tells us, are not carnal. In other words, they are not "according to the tradition of men" nor are they "according to the basic principles of the world." Even so, they are mighty "in God" for the pulling down of "strongholds." These "strongholds," according to Paul, are philosophies, arguments, reasonings, concepts, ideas, and every man-made *ism* (i.e., "every high thing") that

---

[1] Colossians 2:8.
[2] See Matthew 21:23-27.

exalts itself against the "knowledge of God." Primarily, this knowledge of God is derived from just one source: the Bible.

In the very first verse of the Bible, we are told: "In the beginning God created the heavens and the earth." In this simple and uncomplicated sentence are concepts with the most profound implications. If one believes this sentence to be divinely inspired truth, then it completely destroys the "strongholds" of atheism, polytheism, materialism, and pantheism.

Genesis 1:1 says the atheist is definitely wrong when he says there is no God, because Elohim (the name used to identify God in this verse and one that suggests His triune nature) identifies Himself as the Creator. This one true God (viz., the one and only state of being divine, which the Bible tells us is shared by the Father, Son, and Holy Spirit) is contrasted with all the false gods of polytheism.

Furthermore, materialism, a theory that says physical matter is the only fundamental reality and that all being, processes, and phenomena can be explained as manifestations or results of matter, is thoroughly defeated by the divinely revealed truth of Creation. The heavens and the earth, with all the matter contained therein, were simply spoken into existence by Almighty God.

Finally, the transcendent God identified in Genesis 1:1, the One who had, and continues to have, an existence apart from His Creation, is contrasted with the pantheistic concept that teaches God consists of the forces and laws of the universe. In other words, instead of the Biblical concept of a God who is different from His Creation, the pantheist sees God and the Creation as being One. Specifically, such a pantheistic belief is identified as "Monism" (viz., "All is One").

The Christian must not ignore Paul's warning about the doctrines of men or vain philosophy. According to Paul, vain philosophy is a brigand that, if we are not careful, will take us captive and steal from us our spiritual possessions. Deception, long the technique of those who would cheat and steal, is the major device of all man-made philosophy. Promising everything, it delivers nothing; claiming to be one thing, it turns out to be something else entirely!

Unfortunately, many Christians, living at the dawn of the twenty-first century, have either forgotten Paul's warning or no longer believe it. For whatever reasons, Christians, because of their ignorance, have been seduced into thinking that man-made philosophies are religiously neutral. Seemingly unaware of the paradigm of idolatry, they have become enchanted by the smorgasbord of secular thought that obscures the way, perverts the truth, and totally wrecks one's spiritual life. These must be reminded that it was Jesus who said: "I am the way, the truth and the life."[3] What this means is that apart from the way, there is no going; apart from the truth there is no knowing; and apart from the life, there is no spiritual living. This, quite frankly, is why the apostle Paul said that "every thought" must be brought "into captivity to the obedience of Christ."

In Colossians 3:17, Paul wrote that everything one does in "word or deed" is to be done "in the name of the Lord" (i.e., by the Lord's authority). But how can one's actions be correct if one is not thinking properly? And how can one be thinking properly if one has not brought "every thought into captivity to the obedience of Christ"? Therefore, it is clear the Lord calls upon His disciples to out-think, out-live, and out-die the pagans and humanists around about them.

All man-made philosophies are destined for total defeat. It is, therefore, ludicrous that Christians, who have been "called out of

---

[3] John 14:6.

darkness into His marvelous light,"[4] would want to return again to the "weak and beggarly elements" of this world, symbolized in the Bible as spiritual darkness.[5]

Today, our theological chickens are coming home to roost. Many in churches of Christ are in the process of creating idols for their own destruction.[6] If they don't repent, they will be destroyed for their ignorance of God's Word.[7] As the Lord's own unique and special people, poised, as we are, at the beginning of the 21st century, we will either reject, resist, and repent of these destructive heresies, or we will be "cut off." As free moral agents, the choice is ours. None of us is immune. Therefore, self-examination is not out of order for anyone, even the devoutest Christians. Remember, whatever is on the throne, whatever controls one's life, is his idol. It may be "mammon"[8]; it may be personal pleasure[9]; it may be one's work or family; it may be drugs; it may be "omnipotent," "infallible" science; or it may be just SELF.[10] Whatever it is, it must be abandoned.

> *Now therefore, fear the Lord, serve Him in sincerity and in truth, and put away the gods which your fathers served on the other side of the River and in Egypt. Serve the Lord! And if it seems evil to you to serve the Lord, choose for yourselves this day whom you will serve, whether the gods which your fathers served that were on the other side of the River, or the gods of the Amorites, in whose land you dwell. But as for me and my house,*

---

[4] 1 Peter 2:9.
[5] See Galatians 4:9; Ephesians 4:17-20; Colossians 1:9-14.
[6] cf. Hosea 8:4.
[7] See Hosea 4:6.
[8] Matthew 6:24.
[9] See Philippians 3:19.
[10] See Daniel 5:23.

we will serve the Lord. So the people answered and said: "Far be it from us that we should forsake the Lord to serve other gods."[11]

---

[11] Joshua 24:14-16.

Index

A

A Brief History of Time, 125.
Abraham, 80, 82, 84, 107.
Adam and Eve, 40.
agape, 28, 105.
Age Of The Earth controversy, 164.
Alexander, R.D., 159.
American Association for the Advancement of Science, 151.
Andrews, Edward, 152.
anthropomorphism, 12.
Apology, Tertullian's, 131-132.
apostasy, 18.
Arianism, 52.
Aristotle, 59.
arrogance, 163.
Asimov, Isaac, 150, 152-153.
Athenians, 11, 51.
Athens, 50.
Atkins, Peter, 150.

B

Baal, 49.
Barr, James, 120.
Barrow, John, 123.
Behe, Michael, 166.
behemoth, 171.
Belz, John, 143.
Bethell, Tom, 157.
Bible study
    few Christians doing it, 19.
Biblical Words for Time, 120.
Big Bang, 122-124, 152, 169.
Blanchard, John, 149.
Brachiosaurus, 171.
Buddhism, 70.

C

Caesar, Augustus, 130, 133.
Calvin, John, 88-89.
Campbell, Alexander, 179-180, 185.
Can Man Live Without God?, 152.
Canaanites, 49.
Carnegie, Dale, 164.
Carpet God, 46.
Chesterton, G.K., 42-43, 149.
Christendom, 161.
Churchanity, 161, 176.
Cicero, 49.
Collinsville church of Christ, 137.
Concilia, the Roman, 133-134.
Constitution, U.S., 147, 160.

Cottrell, Jack, 186.
Craig, William Lane, 123, 125.

D

Dagon, 49.
Darwin On Trial, 166.
Darwin's Black Box, 166.
Davies, Paul, 122.
Declaration of Independence, 60.
Deism, 59-60, 71, 182.
Deism and Natural Religion, 61.
Dembski, William A., 166.
demonology, 39.
depravity, inherited, 42.
dinosaur, 171-172.
Docetism, 52.
Does God Believe In Atheists?, 149.
Domitian, Roman emperor, 132-133.
Dr. Feelgood, the religion of, 63.
Draper, J.W., 150.

E

Ecclesiastical History, 132.
Eden, garden of, 174.
Epicurus, 59.
Eusebius, of Caesarea, 132.
Evolution versus Creation: The Public Evolution Controversy, 159.

F

Felix, Marcus Antonius, Roman procurator, 129.
Festus, Porcius, Roman governor of Judea, 130.
foreknowledge, 11.
Franklin, Benjamin, 60.

G

Galba, Roman emperor, 132.
Gallio, Junius, Roman proconsul of Asia, 129.
Geisler, Norman L., 155.
geologic column, 169, 171.
Gilkey, Langdon, 18.
God is..., 19.
   eternal, 21.
   immutable, 26.
   infinite, 22.
   omnipotent, 25.
   omnipresent, 23.
   omniscient, 24.
   self-existent, 20.
   triune, 29.
God, Science and Evolution, 152.
God's Foreknowledge and Man's Free Will, 77.
Goddard Institute for Space Studies, 125.
Gomorrah, 81, 140.
gospel preachers, 14.

Gould, Stephen Jay, 151-153.
Guinn v. Church of Christ of Collinsville, 138.
Guinness, Os, 44.

H
Hartshorne, Charles, 76.
Harvard University, 151.
Hawking, Stephen, 124.
hedonism, 146.
Heisenberg's indeterminacy principle, 78.
History of the Conflict Between Religion and Science, 150.
Home To Bethage: a Biography of Robert Richardson, 180.
homosexuality, 148.
How to Win Friends and Influence People, 164.
Hoyle, Fred, 123.
Humanist Manifestos I and II, 61.
Humphries, John, 140.
Huxley, Thomas H., 158.

I
Ideas Have Consequences, 139.
idolatry, 13-14.
   a substitute for God, 39.
   can be highly sophisticated, 39.
   counterfeiting of God, 43.
   covetousness as, 13.
   defined, 142.
   flee, 13.
   not just something pagans engage in, 14.
Implication of Evolution, 158.
In The Beginning, 150.
Institutes of Ecclesiastical History, 128.
Intelligent Design: The Bridge Between Science & Theology, 166.

J
Jastrow, Robert, 125.
Jefferson, Thomas, 60.
Johnson, Phillip E., 166.
Judas, 86.

K
Katrina, hurricane, 144-145, 148.
Kerkut, G.K., 158.
Keyes, Richard, 44.
knowledge
   salvation not possible without, 17.

L
Lanier, Roy H., Sr., 189.
Law of Contradiction, logic's, 124.
lesbianism, 148.

Lewontin, Richard, 151.
Linde, Andrei, 123.
Linnaeus, Carl, 156.
Locke, John, 179, 182.
Logos, 35, 106, 108.

M

Maker of Heaven and Earth, 18.
materialism, 146.
McClean Opinion, 156.
miracles, 185.
modus operandi, 176.
Molech, 47.
Monism, 197.
Morris, Henry M., 168.
Mosheim, Johann Lorenz von, 128.
Mt. Olympus, 59.

N

narcissism, 145.
Nash, Ronald, 75.
naturalism
    philosophical, 156.
Nature and the Greeks, 153.
Nero, Roman emperor, 132-133.
New Orleans, 143, 148.
New York Review of Books, 151.
New York Times, 125.
Newton, Sir Isaac, 61.

niceness, 161.
No God But God, 44.

O

old-earth creationists (OECs), 167, 170-176.
Omnipotence and Other Theological Mistakes, 76.
Otho, Roman emperor, 132.
Overton, Judge William R., 154-156.
Oxford University, 150.

P

pacifists, 161.
Paine, Thomas, 60.
Panentheism, 75, 197.
Pantheism, 113.
pax Romana, 130.
Pentecostalism, 69, 112-113.
Persia, prince of, 115.
Philistines, 49.
Pilate, Pontius, 128.
pluralism, 147.
Praetorian Guard, 132.
pride, 163.
Process Theology, 75.
Puritans, 61.

R

re:thinking magazine, 183.
Reagan, Ronald, 140.

Reasonable Faith, 123.
Religion And Science, 149.
Religion in the Development of American Culture, 62.
Reports on Progress in Physics, 123.
Restoration Movement, 180, 185.
Rice, Richard, 77, 90-91, 94.
Richardson, Dr. Robert, 179-180.
Russell, Bertrand, 149.

S

Sadducees, 69, 182.
Samaritan woman, 18.
Schaeffer, Francis, 149, 154.
Scheme of Redemption, 95-96.
Schrödinger, Erwin, 153.
Scientism, 150, 154, 160.
Seel, John, 44.
September 11th, 148.
Shammah, 185.
Sodom, 81, 140.
Spengler, Oswald, 139.
Spurgeon, Charles, 49.
Strong, Augustus H., 61.
Strong's Greek and Hebrew Lexicon, 97.
Supreme Court, U.S., 129.
Sweet, William Warren, 62.
Swinburne, Richard, 90-91, 94.

Systema Naturae, 156.

T

Tawney, R.H., 60.
teleological argument, 19.
Tertullian, anglicized of Quintus Septimius Florens Tertullianus, 131.
 Tertullian, 132.
The Acquisitive Society, 60.
The Age of Reason, 60.
The American Heritage Dictionary, 55.
The American Spectator, 157.
The Anthropic Cosmological Principle, 123.
The Biblical Doctrine Of The Trinity, 35.
The Christian & War, 161.
The Church At The End Of The Twentieth Century, 149.
The Coherence of Theism, 90.
The Creator In The Courtroom, 155.
The Genesis Flood, 168.
The Kalam Cosmological Argument, 125.
The Study of Time III, 123.
The Sunday Telegraph, 151.
The Timeless Trinity, 190.
The Treasury of David, 49.
Thermodynamics

First Law of, 124.
Second Law of, 124.
Thinking Clearly About God and Science, 153.
Thomas, the apostle, 36.
Tipler, Frank, 123.
Titus, Roman emperor, 132.
Trinity, economic and ontological, 32.

U
uniformitarianism, 169.
University of London, 152.
University of Michigan, 159.

V
Vespasian, Roman emperor, 132.
Vitellius, Roman emperor, 132.

W
Waring, Graham, 61.
Watson v. Jones, 129.
Weaver, Richard M., 139.
Wells, Wayne, 182-183.
What The Bible Says About God The Ruler, 186.
Whitcomb, John C., 168.
Whitehead, Alfred North, 75.
World Magazine, 143.
worship, true
   in Spirit and in truth, 18.

Y
young-earth creationists (YECs), 167, 170, 172, 176.

Z
Zacharias, Ravi, 152.

Other Books By Allan Turner

The Christian & War (ISBN: 0-9777350-0-1)
The Christian & War E-book (ISBN: 0-9777350-1-X)

Allan Turner's Personal Web Site

www.allanturner.com

ALLANITA PRESS PUBLISHING

www.allanitapress.com

www.ingramcontent.com/pod-product-compliance
Ingram Content Group UK Ltd.
Pitfield, Milton Keynes, MK11 3LW, UK
UKHW041429180426
11947UKWH00007B/360